AUGUST 21st
The Rape of Czechoslovakia

BY COLIN CHAPMAN
Foreign News Editor, The Sunday Times

WITH ON THE SPOT REPORTS FROM PRAGUE
By MURRAY SAYLE
Special Correspondent of The Sunday Times

CASSELL LONDON

CASSELL & COMPANY LTD
35 Red Lion Square, London WC1
Melbourne, Sydney, Toronto
Johannesburg, Auckland

SBN 304 93330 9

*Printed in Great Britain by Cox & Wyman Ltd,
London, Reading and Fakenham*

F. 1068

INTRODUCTION

This book is the first detailed account of the Russian intervention in Czechoslovakia. Because of the unusual nature of the conflict the facts filtered out slowly, making it difficult for newspapers to piece together a narrative. The book had to be written quickly, but it is only to a small degree based on newspaper clippings. Murray Sayle in Prague elaborated on his vivid reports in the *Sunday Times* and *The Times* to give readers the atmosphere of the dramatic days following the Russian invasion. Investigations in Britain and Europe by Patricia de Joux have provided an interesting insight into the background and personalities of Alexander Dubcek and the economic reformer, Professor Ota Sik. There is also much new incidental information, not previously published.

I would also like to thank the following for their help: Antony Terry, Chief European Correspondent of the *Sunday Times*, who has visited Prague several times this year and was at Bratislava for the crucial summit meeting in July; Don Berry; Gabriel Ronay, the well-known Soviet commentator who studied Marxist–Leninism and writes on Russian affairs in the *New Statesman* under the name of Gabriel Lorence; Lord Bethell, who has a special knowledge of East Europe; Lancaster University, which is opening Britain's first centre specializing in Czechoslovakia; a large number of Czechoslovak journalists and academics who have been interviewed but who prefer, for obvious reasons, to remain anonymous because they hope one day to return to their country.

COLIN CHAPMAN

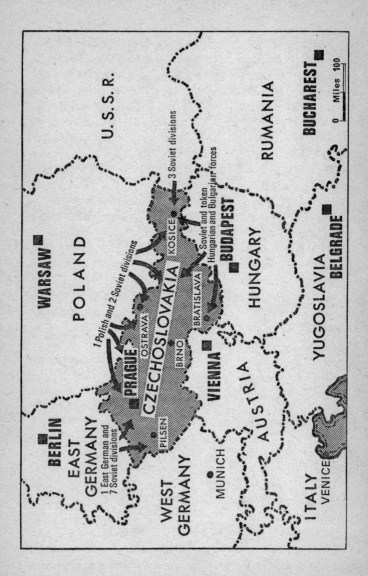

1 INVASION

Ruzyne Airport, Prague, on a drab plateau seven miles from the city centre, is like most international airports in Central Europe. During the daylight hours its runways are congested as inter-city jets carry businessmen, politicians and engineers from capital to capital. At night there is a relative calm, and the chilly evening of August 20 was no exception. An Ilyushin from the Polish airline LOT taxied away and lumbered off into the night heading for Warsaw. The Czech traffic controllers in the tower relaxed; the next scheduled flight, bound for Ankara, was not due for three hours—after midnight; but at ten-thirty a heavy Russian Antonov civil airplane was expected, by special arrangement with Aeroflot, the Soviet airline. This was not particularly surprising to the airport officials, for the same plane had come to Prague the day before under a similar arrangement. On the stroke of ten-thirty the AN24 heaved down from the sky and rolled to a standstill beside the terminal building. A group of men, some in Russian Army uniform, clambered down, strode to waiting cars, and drove off. There was nothing exceptional in that.

Meanwhile in the tatty departure lounge of the terminal building a group of men with holiday gear were slouched in the chairs, smoking heavily and sipping dark coffee, as a cleaner swept the floor around them. They were apparently awaiting the flight to Turkey. Suddenly they all stood up together, took revolvers from their pockets, left two men on guard and disappeared. At this point a number of Russian Volga cars roared up and screeched to a standstill. Their occupants got out, marched quickly back to the stationary AN24 parked on the apron, and went inside it. This was a surprise to the traffic controllers, who had not expected the Russian aircraft to take off until the next morning, but hardly had their surprise registered when their door opened and the 'tourists' who had been sitting in the departure lounge burst in, held them up at pistol point and ordered them to cease to man the radar and talkdown apparatus. As the Czech controllers wondered what was going on, another transporter descended from the pitch black sky, followed minute after minute by a constant stream of aircraft.

The truth at once dawned on the traffic controllers: the Soviet aircraft had been directed into Prague by a special crew operating electronic equipment in the AN24.

Then came the roar of fighters, as Russian MIGs, flying in close formation, screamed over the city, drawing late-night drinkers and dancers to hotel windows to watch. Minutes later Ruzyne Airport was completely under the control of the invaders, as still more planes droned in. Command headquarters were set up for Red Army General Pavlovsky, and infantrymen bearing torches in one hand and sub-machine-guns in the other marched in a long column towards the city. The men were mainly Asiatics, Kalmyk or Mongol, single-minded, brutal soldiers who are often used by the Soviet Army to carry out the more dangerous or unpleasant tasks. Many of them do not even speak Russian. Immediately behind them came tanks and armoured vehicles. As the heavy transports landed, other Red Army marines and parachutists were dropped in the Prague suburb of Sporilov alongside a new section of motorway. The tank columns which entered the city from the airport down the four-lane Lenin Highway split into three at the Square of the October Revolution in Deyvice on the outskirts of the city, one column going south to the Hradcany Palace while the largest column went eastwards to the Prime Minister's office and the third crossed the Vltava River at the Hlavek Bridge, where by 4.30 a.m. several dozen Russian tanks surrounded the Central Committee headquarters. The tanks rumbled across the bridge over the Vltava River and into Wenceslas Square, where engineers had been building a pedestrian subway and so the centre was closed except to trams. But the Russians ignored the signs and rushed straight in. The infantrymen spread out and secured key installations: the crucial bridges over the Vltava; the main roads. It was a model operation, conducted with remorseless efficiency.

It was the same story all over the country. Polish MIGs arrived to set up a base at Tardubice Airfield, forty miles from Prague, and at other military airports all over the country. Sometimes the MIGs came before the troop-carrying transporters. At Hradec Kralove, in north-east Bohemia, a lone MIG15 touched down, a high-ranking Russian officer climbed out, refused to give his name, and would not state the reason for his arrival. The reason became apparent to the base commanding officer later in the day when forty other MIGs had landed, followed by helicopters carrying Russian and Polish soldiers. And, as the aircraft flew in, Moscow gave the orders to ground forces waiting behind the borders of Czechoslovakia to invade. Across they came—into the orchards of Bohemia, into Slovakia from Hungary, into the northern industrial city of Ostrava. The tanks smashed down anything that stood in their way—telegraph poles, trees, even cars parked in the streets. In the east, heavy transport from the Ukraine crossed the frontier. By dawn the first land-bound troops had reached Prague, and joined forces with the élite group of specially trained commandos which had taken Ruzyne Airport. There was no resistance; there could not be. And at 1.10 a.m. on Wednesday, August 21, came this announcement from Prague Radio:

'To the entire people of the Czechoslovak Socialist Republic.

'Yesterday, on August 20, at about 2300, troops of the Soviet Union, the Polish People's Republic, the German Democratic Republic [East Germany], the Hungarian People's Republic and the Bulgarian People's Republic, crossed the frontiers of the Czechoslovak Socialist Republic. This happened without the knowledge of the President of the Republic, the Chairman of the National Assembly, the Prime Minister, or the First Secretary of the Czechoslovak Communist Party Central Committee. In the evening hours the Praesidium of the Czechoslovak Communist Party Central Committee had held a session and discussed preparations for the Fourteenth Czechoslovak Communist Party congress. The Czechoslovak Communist Party Central Committee Praesidium appeals to all citizens of our republic to maintain calm and not to offer resistance to the troops on the march. Our Army, security corps, and people's militia have not received the command to defend the country. The Czechoslovak Communist Party Central Committee Praesidium regard this act as contrary not only to the fundamental principles of relations between socialist states but also as contrary to the principles of international law.'

It was five past seven, American time, on a balmy Washington Tuesday evening, when Mr Dobryin called the White House, and was put through to President Johnson's special assistant for national security, Mr Walt Rostow, who was working in his office in the basement. Dobryin told Rostow that he had a message from Moscow that he wanted to give personally to the President. Mr Dobryin was invited round, but the White House knew what was happening. Earlier that day Johnson had received reports and reconnaissance pictures of large-scale refuelling of Soviet military transport in the Ukraine. There was a report from NATO headquarters in Brussels, presenting the West German Intelligence Service's claim that the recent large-scale Warsaw Pact manœuvres had been only a front for a possible invasion. The Germans had an extensive intelligence network operating inside the Iron Curtain countries; and along their border with Czechoslovakia they were also making use of electronic listening devices similar to those employed by the United States in the demilitarized zone in Vietnam. This sensitive equipment on that Tuesday registered unusually active movement.

Mr Dobryin, punctual as ever, arrived at the White House at eight. He exchanged small talk for a few moments with Mr Rostow, and then greeted the President with a smile. Together, they entered the Cabinet Room; the Soviet Ambassador sat down on one side of the table, Mr Johnson and Mr Rostow on the other. All the usual courtesies were observed; Mr Dobryin was offered, and accepted, a drink. Then the Russian began to read quickly from a long, prepared statement.

Troops of the Soviet Union and four of its Warsaw Pact allies, said Mr Dobryin, had entered Czechoslovakia in fraternal response to an appeal by Czechoslovak 'Party and Government leaders', and they had done so because Communist rule had fallen under heavy attack from counter-revolutionary forces and forces 'hostile to socialism'. The action was an internal action of the Soviet Union, and their own affair.

Mr Dobryin left. Mr Johnson called a special emergency meeting of the National Security Council for ten o'clock, and sent an urgent message to Secretary of State Dean Rusk, who was testifying on Vietnam before the Democratic Platform Committee at the Statler Hilton Hotel. But the President's messenger was beaten to it, and the Secretary of State first learned of the invasion from a note sent to him. Mr Rusk immediately broke off, saying: 'I didn't think I would have to leave immediately when I came, but I think I will have to go and see what this is all about.' Back at the White House

5

contact was made with the American Embassy in Prague, and all the agency reports were studied. The 10 p.m. meeting was followed by a quarter of an hour session at the State Department between Mr Rusk and Mr Dobryin, who was called by phone and arrived within minutes by chauffeur driven car at the Department's basement entrance. The meeting was short and to the point: Rusk read the Ambassador a strongly worded U.S. protest.

By this time the news was pouring into the world's capitals. In Britain both Prime Minister Wilson and Foreign Secretary Michael Stewart were away—Wilson in the Isles of Scilly and Stewart in Dorset. They hurried back to London, a Cabinet meeting was called at 10 Downing Street, and Parliament was recalled. Mr Wilson discussed the crisis over the transatlantic telephone with Lord Caradon, Britain's representative at the UN, who was asked to make a strong statement. Subsequently there was much bluster at the United Nations, but sadly, as usual, no effective action.

Most crimes take place at night, and that night, as they slept, the Czechs and the Slovaks had their country stolen away from them. The marauders sent by Moscow no longer slipped in by stealth; they continued to crunch boldly in astride their tanks. By the time the people were awake and ready to go about their business, troops were in all strategic positions in the streets. Instead of their morning newspaper, the people received clumsily worded leaflets in Russian informing them that their 'brothers' had been called in to liberate them from 'the counter-revolutionaries and imperialists'.

The easiest of the invading army's task should have been the occupation of Slovakia. Its capital Bratislava is only a few kilometres from the Hungarian border, and the Soviet tanks were able to enter the city an hour or so after the orders from Moscow were given. Certainly Russian commanders did not expect to meet the resistance, active and passive, from the Slovaks that eventually hit them. Slovakia is closer to Russia than to Bohemia in language, history and culture, and many Russians thought that Slovak nationalism had been well diluted by its large Hungarian, Ukrainian, gipsy and Jewish minorities. Its population is a mere four and a half million. True, Dubcek and Gustav Husak, the Slovak Communist Party Secretary, were Slovaks, but so was Vasil Bilak, Czechoslovakia's arch-conservative. It is he who is thought to have told the Russians that opposition to their invasion would be less in Slovakia. On the basis of his advice, the Red Army decided to send three armies into Bohemia and only one into Slovakia, correctly calculating that the Czech-speaking regions were more pro-Western.

But even if the Russians had predicted trouble with the Slovaks—and the fact that they occupied the Bratislava Hospital as a priority is evidence that they expected some resistance and some bloodshed—they must have been fairly confident that there would be no bother with the Hungarian minorities. Many of the Hungarians live in the eastern Slovakian town of Roznava, north of the Hungarian border and close to Kosice; in fact almost all the people in Roznava are of Hungarian descent. So the Soviet High Command decided to send Hungarian troops (under their orders because of the Warsaw Pact) into Roznava, and assured them that they would receive a warm welcome when they arrived to defend their countrymen from the 'counter-revolutionaries'. The Hungarian invaders were stunned with surprise when, instead of being greeted with smiles, they were booed and spat at, in some cases by their own relatives. They asked for food—they had not taken much because they expected it would be provided by their 'fellow-countrymen'—but it was refused, as was water, and other facilities. Finally the Hungarian colonel went to see the Mayor of Roznava, and the two of them worked out an agreement. There was a large technical school in the town that was not being used because the students, miners from a nearby colliery, were on holiday. The soldiers were told they could live and sleep there and be supplied with plenty of food and water, on one condition: that they obeyed the curfew like everyone else. The Mayor insisted that after nightfall every soldier would have to be inside the school, and the door locked. The Mayor himself kept the key and promptly each morning at dawn he went round to the school and let them out for inspection.

In Bratislava a sullen crowd gathered in the main streets, resignation and despair in their faces. Some sat down in a vain attempt to block the onsurge of tanks; then scrambled desperately away as it became clear that a few dead bodies would not prevent their passage. The women formed queues at the provision shops, hoarding food in expectation of shortage. The Slovak Minister of Trade introduced rationing, which restricted purchases to a maximum of four pounds of flour, half a pound of rice, one pound of sugar, one pound of meat and sausage meat, a quarter of a pound of butter, five eggs, and one piece of soap. Girls hitched up their miniskirts and posed saucily to distract the soldiers; as they did so Slovak youths darted in and out amid the tanks and troop lorries, smashing headlights with stones, wrenching open doors, and filching oil drums. They set some of the drums alight, and one tank was shrouded in smoke, with its occupants choking over their machine-guns. While the pall lingered over it, the youths tried to stop it from moving on by dumping paving stones in front of its tracks; but the tank just edged forward, crushed the stone to powder, and rumbled on. Some of the older people tried to reason with the Russian soldiers, telling them they were not wanted, and asking them to return home. Most of the steel-helmeted troops looked perplexed, but unconcerned; those that answered the questioning and the taunting crowd—sometimes quietly hostile, sometimes hissing with anger—replied that they were merely acting under instructions.

The invaders were under strong orders to show restraint. Czechoslovak Radio reported that the commanders of the Warsaw Pact troops had been told: 'Do not permit attempts to disarm Czechoslovak units. Leave areas where Czechoslovak troops are stationed. Leave small towns—and station yourselves outside them. In large cities deploy yourselves in parks and open spaces, and do not disrupt the public traffic. Ensure that allied troops are supplied from your own stores.'

Considering the severe provocation under which they were put, the occupying soldiers—many of them youths in their late teens—exercised quite remarkable restraint, reflecting the rigid discipline of the Red Army. Sometimes their nerve snapped, but not often. When it did, blood flowed, and bitterness turned to hate.

Sometimes death occurred almost by accident. In Bratislava students gathered on the steps of the university to watch the green tanks clank across the Danube from the Hungarian border, and rumble through the streets of the Slovak capital. One of them was a 15-year-old student nurse, and she watched as a crowd of men and boys hurled first abuse and then chunks of brick at the Soviet troops. Suddenly there was a shot fired towards the crowd by a soldier squatting on the back of a tank. The girl slumped to the ground, and died within seconds. The crowd reacted with stunned shock, and then there was a torrent of insults and more bricks. The soldier fired again, and again; that way four other people died.

A few hours later the story was told, simply but poignantly, in thick gold letters scrawled on the stone walls of the Faculty of Philosophy: 'Here Russian occupiers killed a girl. She was 15. August 21, 1968.'

9

2 THE STRUGGLE FOR FREEDOM

August 21, 1968—the invasion. It meant the end of almost $7\frac{1}{2}$ months of freedom for the stolid Czechoslovaks, $7\frac{1}{2}$ months in which middle-aged party functionaries, bearded students, and housewives in shabby raincoats had together carried ahead their own revolution and fight for freedom. It was $7\frac{1}{2}$ months of heady excitement for a people who in history have always been reasonable, unheroic, realistic, and calm. It was a new-style revolution, uncompromising in its desire to reverse as quickly as possible the drab conformist policies of the former Party Secretary Antonin Novotny, but totally without violence. This short revolution was not one of passion, but one of passionate reasonableness —reflecting all the time the Czechs' loathing of bloodshed. Yet, sadly, it seems that history has ordered that Czechoslovakia should remain a country under someone else's influence. The remarkable prediction of the great Czech historian Frantisek Palacky is particularly interesting. He argued that the western Slavonic peoples could not stand alone against the terrific pressure from Panslavic Russians on one side and the Pangermanistic Prussians on the other. A Central European Federation, even under the Habsburgs, was essential for stability. 'If Austria [the Austrian Empire] did not exist it would have to be created in the interests of Europe and humanity.' Time after time, attempts by the Czechs and the Slovaks to assert themselves as independent peoples have been thwarted. The Russians are not the only culprits. For centuries the Czechs and the Slovaks were persecuted and cruelly ill-treated by the Germans and the Hungarians who dominated the Austrian empire of the Habsburgs. After World War I, the Czechs and Slovaks gained their national freedom and the Democratic Czechoslovak Republic was proclaimed on October 28, 1918. Only twenty years later Britain and France sold the Czechoslovaks down the river. At Munich they made an agreement with Hitler whereby Czechoslovakia was deprived of its borderland. Then, on March 15, 1939, the country was occupied by the Nazi Wehrmacht. The Nazis ruthlessly exploited their occupation and impoverished the Czech nation. Some two million Czechs served as slaves in the war industry, and about 360,000 people fell in the fighting, or died in the foul German concentration camps.

In 1945 Czechoslovakia was liberated by the Red Army, but it was a liberation without real freedom. A year earlier, the country's future had already been decided by an arrangement to split Europe into 'spheres of influence'—the East, dominated by the Soviet Union and Moscow, and the West, dominated by America, Britain, France, and later a rebuilt West Germany. That key decision was made, not at Yalta as many have suggested, but in Moscow. On May 5, 1944, when the Russians were still inside their own frontiers, an informal deal was made between Churchill and Stalin. On a desk in Stalin's study in the Kremlin, there was a map of Europe, on which the pre-war countries were rationed out between East and West. It is said that Stalin ticked them off with a blue crayon. Greece was assigned to the West, Rumania and Bulgaria were put on Russia's side, while Hungary and Yugoslavia were divided between the two. Later at Yalta, Czechoslovakia was barely mentioned, except that it was labelled as a liberated state where there would be free elections. The United States deny it, but there has never been much doubt that Czechoslovakia was one of those countries said to be within the 'Soviet sphere of influence', while in 1946, Winston Churchill sat beside President Truman in Fulton, Missouri, and declared that 'from Stettin in the Baltic to Trieste in the Adriatic, an Iron Curtain has descended upon Europe. Behind that line lie all the capitals of the ancient states of Central and Eastern Europe—Warsaw, Berlin, Prague, Vienna, Budapest, Belgrade, Bucharest and Sofia. All these famous cities and the populations around them lie in what I must call the Soviet sphere.'

In the early post-war years, between 1945 and 1948, there was great hope that the new Czechoslovak Republic would rid itself of the mistakes and injustices —both in social and nationalistic questions—of the pre-Munich days, and would build itself up into a real democracy. The elections in 1946 were held under democratic conditions, and the fact that the Communist Party won about 38 per cent of the total votes was sufficient proof of the importance of the Communists and their popular policies. But the 'People's Policy' of the Czechoslovak Communists was one thing and the great power policies of Stalin another. It was not long before the crucial confrontation came. Early in 1948, just after Yugoslavia had been expelled from the Soviet bloc, Czechoslovakia faced pressure from Moscow to conform with the views of the Kremlin.

Stalin forced the Czechoslovak Communists to renounce participation in the Marshall Plan, to break off the coalition with the non-Communists in the Government, and then, after the *coup d'état* in February 1948, to accept wholly the Soviet-style rule with all its consequences (bureaucratic Party rule, land collectivization, rigid economic planning, a sharpening of the class war with spectacular purges and show trials, etc.).

There followed nearly twenty years of hard-line Communism, and the drab life that entailed. But, at the 13th Congress of the Czechoslovak Communist Party in June 1966, there was a new electric excitement in the air. Plans were afoot to introduce a radical new economic policy. The Czechoslovaks, with the most advanced economy in Eastern Europe, had begun to notice that their standard of living was lagging behind countries like Poland and Hungary. They resented this greatly, particularly because Czechoslovakia was well capitalized with heavy industry, and was a highly competitive industrial nation, unlike other countries in the Soviet bloc. It was this new Czechoslovak economic plan conceived by Professor Ota Sik that went totally against Moscow's rigid thinking (Professor Sik is a key figure in the crisis; he is discussed at length in Chapter Eight). Nevertheless, Professor Sik was allowed to experiment with his new ideas. Another important concession Novotny's old guard made at the 1966 Congress was in the even more sensitive field of ideology. They agreed that a working party would draft a paper on the correct role of the Communist Party, based on a return to true Leninism. It was accepted, in theory, that this might lead to the Leninist doctrine of a separation of State and Party. What Novotny never dreamed of was that in practice it would lead to the separation of his two jobs as boss of the Party and Head of State. But even these developments need not have led to a revolution, had Novotny and his men been more sophisticated about the intellectuals. The latter were already deeply alienated from the regime, particularly because of its persistent anti-Semitism. The writer Ladislav Mnacko wrote a book called *The Taste of Power*, with an open attack on Novotny. It was submitted to the censor who, in ordering certain passages to be struck out, forgot to say that it must be re-submitted. Mnacko promptly deleted the passages and sent his manuscript to Fritz Molden, a publisher in Vienna. Later he fled the country and went to Israel in a blaze of publicity.

This was followed by an extremely stormy 4th Congress of Czechoslovak writers, at which the intellectuals angrily demanded freer contact with the rest of the world. They seemed passionately concerned with simple things—justice, truth, and human dignity. And they said they were beginning to doubt the ability of the

13

Communist Party to renew itself from within, encourage excellence, and adapt itself to modern times. They wanted open debate, and said plainly that they felt that the Party's attempts to dictate opinion and suppress open discussion were no longer appropriate to a sophisticated country facing complex problems never dreamed of by Marx or Lenin. The Fourth Writers' Congress was of exceptional importance. During its session, Kohout read the Soljenitzyn letter addressed to Russian writers to stand firm against oppression; Klima, in an ironic speech, pointed out that there had been more press freedom a hundred years earlier in the Imperial Constitution of Austria than under Novotny's press laws; and the popular writer Ludovik Vaculik provided a climax with a telling oration about the abuse of power. The congress ended with an open revolt against the chief Party ideologist present, Jiri Hendrych, who, feeling he was no longer in charge, stalked out in a fit of fury. His last words were: 'Thus you have lost everything.' As a punishment, three leading Communist writers, all progressives—Liehm, Klima, and Vaculik—were expelled from the C.C.P. The Union of Czech Writers' weekly paper, *Literarni Noviny*, was banned until a new editor was found. But this achieved little for the Party diehards; under the administration of the new mediocre executives the paper was boycotted by the majority of its readers. Vast numbers of unsold copies piled up in news kiosks. At this time the ferment in Czechoslovakia was little known in the outside world, and indeed it may never have come into the open with such force but for a curious document. This was an outspoken and abusive 1,000-word 'manifesto' of Czechoslovak writers. The document was purported to have been signed by 183 writers, 69 artists, 21 film and television people, 56 scientists and other intellectuals, and it appealed to popular world opinion for moral support in the writers' struggle against censorship and victimization in Czechoslovakia. It accused Mr Novotny and Communist Party leaders in Prague of carrying out 'a witchhunt of pronounced fascist character', and the state of employing terrorist methods against writers. The document was well written, terse and lucid. It called upon well known names for help—Bertrand Russell, Arthur Miller, John Steinbeck, Jean-Paul Sartre, John Osborne, Günther Grasse, and others. Its contents were published in the *Sunday Times* on September 3, 1967, and it was reprinted all round the world in the leading papers of the United States, Europe, and Australasia. It caused a sensation. In Prague and elsewhere the document was immediately labelled as a hoax. Certainly it was not what it claimed to be, for later inquiries revealed that the manifesto had not been signed by all those originally claimed as supporting it. Dr Ivan Pfaff, the Czech historian, admitted drafting the text, and on leaving prison after being held on charges of 'disrupting the public' admitted that he had estimated how many and which writers and other people might approve of his proclamation. However, though the document was not as genuine as it seemed, it clearly was an expression of a widespread state of mind among the Czechoslovak intelligentsia, who could not speak out for fear of reprisals.

Suddenly world attention was focused on Czechoslovakia, and it was clear that Novotny's first mistake was to stir up the beehive of the intellectuals. He followed it up with yet another blunder, one which was even more important. It happened when the plenum of the Central Committee were about to meet on October 30 to discuss the report of the working party on the role of the Communist Party.

Early on the bitterly cold evening of the day preceding the meeting, in the students' hostel at Strahow, the electricity failed and the students were plunged into darkness. This was the last straw. Their morale was low anyway. Too many of them could look forward after years of studying to earning less as engineers and doctors than they would be getting if they had gone straight into a factory at the age of fifteen. In the spirit of a rag, rather than a riot, they organized a candlelight procession and marched into the city. At the medieval market place they came up against the police riot squad. There was some scuffling, but the students eventually dispersed. The police released most of those they had arrested, but not all. When the students got back to Strahow and found that two of their number were still being held a real riot broke out. The police were called up again and things got nasty; there was no shooting, but the scene presaged those in Paris and Chicago in the summer of 1968; tear gas was used and bones were broken with police truncheons and pistol butts.

Antonin Novotny then made the third and perhaps the most serious blunder of all and in so doing alienated all possibility of support from the Slovaks. The Slovaks are only $4\frac{1}{2}$ million of the 14 million Czechoslovakian people; they have a birth rate two or three times as high as the Czechs and they have been grossly misused by the economic planners of Prague. (The Czechs were still inclined to make jokes about 'primitive Slovaks'.) In the town of Martin, perched high on the Western slopes of the Carpathians, is the headquarters of the 150-year-old, twice suppressed organization called Matica Slovenska, which roughly translated means 'Little Mother of the Slovaks'. Officially, it was no more than a sort of Arts Council for Slovak culture, yet in many ways it was at that time the most politically significant place in Slovakia. Slovenska's librarian, Ian Irmler, treasures a hand-inscribed album of Slovak manuscripts, dedicated on its front page to 'Comrade Antonin Novotny during his visit to Matica Slovenska'. Inside the album is tucked a postal rejection slip signed in Novotny's own hand. 'Sent back—addressee does not wish to receive.'

Only four months later the Communists in the nearby textile town of Trencin made the first grass roots move against the Party leader. On December 23, the local Party Secretary called five hundred officials to a secret meeting in a cinema. They decided that Novotny would have to go. Shortly afterwards they sent a full petition to the Slovak Party Secretary—an almost unknown man called Dubcek—for Novotny's removal, primarily on the grounds of his insulting attitude to the Slovaks. One Trencin man asked for a knife to sign the Dubcek petition with his blood, while less dramatically Catholic priests produced the petition in their pulpits.

So just after the glorious anniversary of the great October Revolution, the great Novotny regime was in glorious trouble. The Old Guard was not interested in Slovakia. The Old Guard refused to believe that the students were excited over anything more than a power failure—and everyone in Czechoslovakia was used to power failures. Even before the Slovak petition arrived Novotny was already in deep water in Prague. In November, the Praesidium met to consider the plan for reform of the party, and 6 out of 10 members with votes were in favour of splitting Novotny's two jobs. Novotny decided to put the question to the plenum, when it met on December 15. Presumably he hoped that in the larger body there were enough henchmen to swamp the rebels. More important it gave him time, which he desperately needed. Reports were coming in from branches telling of the bitter disillusionment of Party members, who felt that the regime had systematically ignored their wishes for a year. The intellectuals' rumblings and the workers' protests grew together into a national crisis. Novotny reacted predictably. He picked up the telephone, called the Kremlin, and spoke to Leonid Breshnev, the Soviet Party boss. Breshnev flew at once to Prague, bringing much needed support to the Stalinist leader.

His visit however achieved very little for Novotny. One member of the Praesidium was persuaded to switch his vote to the Party boss to produce a deadlock at five-five, which was hardly what Novotny wanted. And suddenly there was a new crisis. The plenum of the Central Committee did not meet as expected on December 15, and on December 16 a Czechoslovak armoured division at Brdy began rolling towards Prague, its tanks heading for the heights around the city; other tanks were said to have covered more than a quarter of the distance to Bratislava, the capital of Slovakia. Who brought them in? One of those involved was Major General Jan Sejna, who also ordered a partial mobilization of troops to ensure that 'the Central Committee voted correctly' (Sejna later defected to the United States—the most senior Communist military official to do so since the Cold War began). Another officer involved was Colonel-General Janko, the number two in the Czechoslovak Ministry of Defence (later he shot himself in the chest, was revived on the way to the hospital, but shot himself again and died). The troops never reached the city because General Prchlik warned Dubcek, and the soldiers were sent back to the barracks. There was never an explanation for the manœuvres other than the fact that the troops were carrying out routine training for the parade celebrating the 20th anniversary of the Czech revolution on February 25.

Three days later the session of the full Central Committee met at the Communist headquarters at Prague, and there was a grim and angry confrontation. The question was no longer between one programme or another, or between two ideological interpretations of Marxism-Leninism—it was a naked struggle for power.

The symbolic issue was whether the jobs as Head of State and Party boss, which Novotny held, should be split. The meeting broke up in high drama. A fortnight later the Central Committee met again. Dubcek, Sik, Smrkovsky and the progressives had put the break to good use and on January 5 the vote was unanimous. Novotny was replaced as Party boss by Dubcek. Novotny was allowed to continue for the time being as President and to live in his sumptuous apartments, but a few weeks later he was removed from his office and was replaced by Mr Svoboda.

The defection to the United States of General Sejna, and the reopening of investigations into Mazaryk's death, helped the new leadership to rally popular support and to isolate the hard-line reactionaries. Within a short time literary and press censorship was totally abolished and rehabilitation of victims of Stalinist terror trials was in full swing. Freedom of minority opinion was guaranteed, and travel restrictions were lifted. Then on April 15, 1968, Dubcek's new progressive regime published a 27,000-word Action Programme. The programme was a sensation and must have confirmed Moscow's worst fears. Legislation was being prepared to regulate freedom of the press and the right of assembly; there were to be elections, much fairer elections; legislation was to be introduced to aid the rehabilitation of victims of previous Communist regimes, and the Czech economy was to be reorganized so as to become much more effective in both domestic and Western export markets. There was to be more trade with West Germany.

Opposition to Dubcek moved swiftly. Scurrilous leaflets distributed through the post and at factories attacked Dubcek. Progressive journalists were sent letters threatening execution, 'when we get back to power'. In speeches from the factory floor, Novotny and other conservatives fermented anti-intellectual feelings and openly tried to rally workers and trade union leaders against the new programme, but to little avail. One major difference between the Soviet Union and Czechoslovakia is that most of the workers in Czechoslovakia have always been members of the Communist Party, whereas in the Soviet Union this is something of a privilege reserved for only a selected number. In one Prague factory union leaders called two thousand workers for a short meeting just to ask them if they would pass a ready-made rubber-stamp resolution supporting Dubcek. This was not enough for the workers, who stood up and criticized the union leadership and quoted Kipling in support of humanist ideas. The union leaders sat pale through the two-hour meeting, and watched the men adopt an even more far-reaching resolution calling for a genuine multi-party system and for religious freedom.

On March 23 Dubcek took his plans to the Soviet bloc leaders at a meeting of Warsaw Pact leaders in Dresden, East Germany. The meeting was attended by the three Soviet leaders, Mr Breshnev, Mr Kosygin and Mr Suslov, and by Communist leaders of East Germany, Poland and Hungary. It was obvious it was too late to check the reforms, for Dubcek had the workers behind him.

Dubcek returned from Dresden to Prague and immediately called in the editors of the leading newspapers and asked them to play down the new liberalizing reforms. It was too late. A few weeks later he flew to Moscow to reassure Breshnev of his support for the Soviet bloc. But there were ominous signs that the Soviet Union might be planning to exert force to bring Dubcek to heel. The Kremlin was under pressure from Walter Ulbricht in East Germany, who had already begun to seal off its borders with Czechoslovakia. Bus tours of Czechoslovakia were cancelled, and many official visits were called off. *Volkszeitung*, a German-language Prague newspaper, was banned from circulation throughout most of East Germany. Tension built up. In Moscow the Czechoslovak Ambassador was summoned to the Kremlin for a two-hour tirade from Mr Breshnev. Then Mr Kosygin flew to Prague for 'a short holiday and treatment' and for an 'incidental exchange of views on questions affecting both sides'. At so tense a moment, nobody believed so flimsy an excuse. Kosygin came in fact to give Dubcek a blunt warning: 'Ease the reforms or we shall have to do something more active.'

On May 30 Soviet and Polish troops arrived on Czechoslovakian soil to take part in Warsaw Pact exercises, but even this ominous warning did not halt the progress towards reform, and after the manœuvres ended on June 30, the Soviet troops stayed on, inconspicuous in the woods and fields and on the minor roads. Just behind the border, a Russian force of tanks, guns, mortars and armoured-cars stood waiting. Yet the Slovaks and Czechs seemed to accept that the Russians were fighting a psychological war against them, in which the dawdling withdrawal was only one weapon. In Prague, passers-by were asked to sign petitions protesting against what looked like the Russian threat. On Prikopech, one of the main streets, a middle-aged Czech gave his views about the tense situation: 'It is certainly very exciting,' he said slowly, 'but it makes me feel I have been here before. 1938, 1948, and now 1968. Do you see?'

*　　*　　*

On the evening of May 8 four grim-faced European leaders alighted from their Illyushin aircraft in Moscow, their faces belying the official explanation that they had come to attend the joyful celebrations marking the 23rd anniversary of the defeat of Nazi Germany. Within hours Mr Gomulka of Poland, Herr Ulbricht of East

Germany, Mr Kadar of Hungary, and Mr Zhivkov of Bulgaria, met the Soviet leaders. President Ceausescu of Rumania was not invited to join this secret policy-making gathering of the Communist leaders closest to Moscow in the Warsaw Pact alliance.

A few hours later, Soviet troops stationed in Poland were reported moving towards the Czechoslovak border south of Cracow. Western diplomats and military attaches were forbidden by Polish security forces from leaving Warsaw. East European sources indicated that the Soviet troops seen in southern Poland were about to take part in Warsaw Pact manœuvres in Czechoslovakia; such large-scale manœuvres had indeed been planned, but then were cancelled at Dubcek's request after the Dresden meeting of East European leaders in March.

The Czechoslovak leaders were nonplussed. They had reluctantly agreed to admit allied soldiers into the country, but for staff-level exercises only. But instead of a few signals units and staff officers, the Russians rolled in with tanks, mobile infantry of division strength and enough radio and jamming equipment to blanket Czechoslovakia with Soviet broadcasts. The unbelievable was happening: the Soviet Union was threatening to use its armed forces against a sister socialist country and the Warsaw Pact, conceived as a defensive military alliance 'against West German and American imperialism,' was being turned into an internal police force by Moscow.

Nicolae Ceausescu, the Rumanian Party's First Secretary, and President Tito and other Yugoslav leaders at once came to the defence of Czechoslovakia, challenging Russia's right to use the Warsaw Treaty as an excuse to interfere in Prague's internal affairs. 'When the Warsaw Pact organization was founded, it was conceived as an instrument of collective defence', Mr Ceausescu said in an unexpectedly tough speech for a Rumanian Party leader. 'At no point was it visualized that the Warsaw Treaty could be used to justify interference in the internal affairs of other countries. . . . The Rumanian Communist Party does not share the view of those alarmed over what is allegedly happening in Czechoslovakia and who would like to intervene to force Czechoslovakia onto a particular socialist road.'

The Yugoslavs censured the Soviet threat in the same uncompromising tone, and demanded that Russia should leave the Czechoslovaks alone.

As the Warsaw Pact 'staff-level' exercises in Czechoslovakia got under way in those first days of June, Russian pressure on Mr Dubcek increased. It soon became apparent that the Soviet troops were there ready to support some kind of *coup d'état* by the Stalinist Old Guard. But, contrary to Moscow's expectations, the Russian threat of intervention stiffened the spirit of independence and united the nation around the Czechoslovak Communist Party leaders for the first time in twenty years. Far from weakening the position of Mr Dubcek and his reform-minded colleagues, the Russians succeeded in consolidating it. The Moscow-orientated conservatives failed to stage a *coup* because when it came to the crunch the secret police, the 'Sword of the Working Class', and the workers militia, the mainstay of the old-style regime, forgot their 'internationalist duties' towards the Great Socialist Motherland, and proved more Czech than Communist.

When the manœuvres ended on June 30 the Soviet troops stayed on. The withdrawal of Russian troops had been stopped because of 'abnormal traffic conditions', an embarrassed Czechoslovak Defence Ministry announced. With every passing day it became clearer that the Russians were slowing down the withdrawal of their soldiers. After repeated representations by Prague, Marshal Yakubovsky, the commander of the Warsaw Pact forces, agreed to resume the withdrawal of his troops. But the relief felt by the Czechs and Slovaks was tempered by the now hysterical Soviet, East German and Polish press campaign against the Prague leadership.

Meanwhile, another important development was at hand. Secret letters from the Politburos of the Soviet Party and its four allies were received by the Praesidium of the Czechoslovak Communist Party, containing an invitation to a joint meeting in Warsaw. The Czechoslovak Praesidium politely but firmly declined to attend another summit meeting just to listen to Breshnev's ragings.

After days of Soviet troop movements and rising tensions, the leaders of the Soviet Union and its four loyal allies met in emergency session in Warsaw on July 14 to decide how to deal with the rebellious Dubcek. At the end of their two-day meeting the five Warsaw Pact countries addressed a dramatic letter to the Czechoslovak leadership informing them that continued liberalization was 'absolutely unacceptable'. It will go down in history as the 'Warsaw Letter'.

'We do not want to interfere in your affairs or infringe your sovereignty, but there are forces in Czechoslovakia trying to take the country out of the socialist camp. We will not agree that the historical achievements of Czechoslovakia should be threatened. We will not permit Imperialism to split the socialist camp from inside or from outside, with or without force. There must be no change in the balance of power. In January we believed that you held the situation in control and would take the way of democratic centralism, but you began to ignore this way, which meant that the leading role of the Party was threatened. The word 'democracy' is being misused in Czechoslovakia and there are campaigns against honest Party workers. The aim of these campaigns is to end the leading role of the Party, to undermine socialism, and to turn Czechoslovakia against the other socialist countries. New political organizations are being formed outside the National Front. These are centres of reactionary forces and their aim is to take over power in Czechoslovakia and bring back the bourgeois regime. Anti-socialist and revisionist forces have taken power in the press and all the mass media and use it as a tribune for attacks against the Communist Party and also anti-socialist demagogy designed to undermine friendship with the Soviet Union and the socialist countries. Many mass media exert real moral terror against those who stand firm against reaction. Even after the plenary session in May the attacks got stronger and stronger. Nobody stood up against them. Only in such a situation could a manifesto like 'Two Thousand Words' [Chapter 8] appear. The manifesto was an open attack on the Party and on constitutional power. It was an attempt at anarchy and a platform for counter-revolution.

'The situation is absolutely unacceptable to the socialist countries. The fact that the bourgeois press writes approvingly of developments in Czechoslovakia indicates that the forces of reaction have foreign links. Do you not see this, comrades? Do you think declarations are enough? How can you organize a campaign against the military manœuvres in Czechoslovakia? There is a threat to the vital interests of other socialist countries. Every Communist Party is responsible not only to its own working classes, but to the international working class as well, and we therefore think that the fight against anti-Communist forces, which is necessary to save socialism in Czechoslovakia, is not only your fight but ours too. The defence of the working classes and of all workers requires that the *following four points be observed*:

(1) Mobilization of means at the disposal of a socialist state in the fight against anti-socialist forces;

(2) Ending the activities of all political organizations which fight against socialism;

(3) The Party must hold in its hands all mass media and use them in the interests of the working classes;

(4) The unity of the Party must be maintained on the principles of Marxism–Leninism and democratic centralism in opposition to people who help enemy forces.'

The language of the Warsaw Letter was such that no independent Party could accept it if it wanted to rely on public opinion instead of, as Dubcek had put it, 'discredited bureaucratic-police methods'. Soviet fears, said Dubcek, were unjustified. He did not agree that the Party's leading role was in danger or that freedom of the press needed to be curbed, and argued that most of the troubles were in fact the *result* of bureaucratic centralism. His dignified and calm reply was accompanied by invitations to Breshnev, Gomulka, Ulbricht, Kadar and Zhivkov, to bilateral talks in Czechoslovakia to discuss wider issues, and not only Czechoslovakia. The Russians had been trying to get the Czechoslovak leaders to Kiev, Lvov or Moscow. Mindful perhaps of the fate of the Hungarian General Pal Malater in 1956, lured to Soviet headquarters in Hungary under the pretext of negotiations, and never seen again, Dubcek refused to leave his country. On July 17 Breshnev demanded that the Czechoslovaks agree to a meeting to be held two days later between the entire ruling bodies of the two Parties. He suggested Kosice, a sleepy Slovak city forty-five miles west of the Soviet border as the venue. But the fact that sizeable Soviet forces 'on their way home' happened to have converged on the town, made Kosice a dangerous place, and the venue was rejected.

The simmering crisis came near to boiling over the next week when General Vaclav Prchlik, head of the

Security Department of the Czech Central Committee, suddenly called for an overhaul in the command structure of the Warsaw Pact. There was no reason, the General said, why the commander should always be a Soviet General, nor was there any justification for filling all command posts with Russian officers. He suggested that the top policy-making posts should be held by officers of Warsaw Pact countries in turn, and that the dormant consultative body of the Pact should be revitalized. And he added that there was nothing in the Warsaw Pact Treaty to justify the presence of foreign troops in a country that did not want them. This was, understandably, too much for Moscow.

The Russian reply was to remind Prague tartly that 145,000 soldiers of the Soviet Army laid down their lives to liberate Czechoslovakia during World War II and to ask Prague to allow the stationing of Soviet troops on the Czechoslovak border with West Germany 'to strengthen defences'.

On July 23 matters came to a head. A massive military exercise covering most of Russia's western regions from the Baltic to the Black Sea, including the Czechoslovak border areas, was announced by the Soviet Defence Ministry. Soviet reservists, normally serving the forces as rear support troops, were called up and civilian transport was requisitioned. Marshal Grechko, the Soviet Defence Minister, was recalled from an official visit to Algeria. Russia was obviously ready to use force. The Czechs had to seek a compromise, and agreed to hold talks in Cierna-nad-Tisou in eastern Slovaki, near the Soviet border.

The fact that they were to be held on Czechoslovak soil was seen as an indication that Dubcek's steady nerve had won Czechoslovakia the first round in the Moscow–Prague confrontation. But the unusual stipulation that the Soviet Politburo should meet the entire Praesidium of the Czechoslovak Party was seen as an

27

attempt to split the new-found unity of the Czecho-slovak leaders and to isolate Dubcek. There were good reasons to fear this. The Czechoslovak Party's ruling Praesidium was an oddly assorted alliance between four conservatives, five liberals and two 'waverers' who could tilt the balance either way. The Russians hoped that once removed from the heady liberalizing atmosphere of their capital, the basically conservative Communists would show their true colour. One of them could then be persuaded to form a 'Revolutionary Workers and Peasants Government'—as Janos Kadar, a Minister in Imre Nagy's Government, did in November 1956 to 'justify' the Soviet attack on Budapest.

So on July 28 the Politburo of the Soviet Communist Party, headed by Leonid Breshnev, Premier Kosygin and Nikolai Podgorny, boarded a special train in Kiev to journey to Cierna-nad-Tisou for their confrontation with the Czechoslovaks. The trains of the two sides drew up facing each other about fifty yards apart in front of the Cierna station on the night of July 28. At Soviet insistence the meeting was to take place in complete secrecy. A double ring of Czechoslovak soldiers and police surrounded Cierna to ensure that the press could not get near the trains. The Russians, true to the expected form, took an intransigent stance and not only stuck to the demands set out in the Warsaw Letter but went even farther, adding new stipulations to their lists. The Czechoslovak leaders wanted first and foremost an end to the relentless verbal onslaught on their country. They also demanded assurances that Czechslovak sovereignty would be respected and pressed for the withdrawal of Soviet troops. They showed little inclination to agree to the permanent stationing of Soviet troops on Czechoslovak soil, and reasoned with the Russian leaders to let them carry on their democratization process in peace. At about 11 p.m. when the talks were adjourned and deadlock seemed total, the Russians realized that it was not going to be easy to brow-beat the Czechoslovaks.

Next morning, July 30, President Svoboda made a firm statement reaffirming Czechoslovakia's right to her sovereignty. He also spoke of his country's unwavering loyalty to the socialist commonwealth and the Warsaw Pact. Both delegations took a constitutional stroll before lunch. President Podgorny and Premier Kosygin were seen strolling down the main street in Cierna with President Svoboba and Mr Smrkovsky, the Speaker of the Czechoslovak Parliament, all engrossed in animated conversation. A communique was issued through the official Soviet news agency *Tass* saying the talks were being held in an atmosphere of 'frankness and comradeship'.

At 3 a.m. that night a railwayman saw a solitary man walking up and down Cierna station. It was Mr Dubcek, the Czechoslovak Party leader. The railway worker invited the Party Secretary to the railway offices where other railway workers joined them and talked until nearly 4 a.m. Asked why he had not gone to bed, Mr Dubcek said that he regularly slept only from 3 to 7 a.m., revealing the tremendous physical and mental strain under which he had to work.

While the talks went on the military pressure was increased still more. The Soviet Defence Ministry announced that the 'rear troop exercises' had been extended beyond the borders of the Soviet Union. Soviet troops not normally stationed in Poland under Warsaw Pact provisions were aligned from one end of Poland to the the other. Russian armoured units were reported moving towards the 800-mile-long Polish–Czechoslovak frontier. Polish troops and equipment were also on the move. And in East Germany a large formation of Soviet supply columns was rolling southwards. Travellers reported seeing Russian troops massed in field encampments between Dresden and the Czechoslovak border. Additional anti-aircraft exercises, code-named 'Skyshield', were in full swing. The Soviet press spoke of 'realistic battles' with simulated nuclear explosions taking place. And General Norkov, the second-in-command of the vast manœuvres, was quoted as saying that 'in scope, this is one of the biggest-ever exercises conducted by the Soviet Army'.

The Russians, presumably expecting that something like a *coup* or suitable provocation would take place in Prague, entitling Soviet troops to 'restore order', seemed quite happy to spin out the talks. On the third day, July 31, Breshnev continued his tough line and was full of abuse for his erstwhile friend 'Sasha'—Dubcek's nick-name from his days in Russia. It was Mikhail Suslov, the Soviet Party's chief ideologist and expert on inter-Party affairs, who came to Dubcek's rescue by recalling a discussion in the Soviet Politburo several weeks earlier when the 'forceful approach' towards Czechoslovakia, advocated by East Germany's Ulbricht, was rejected. Breshnev had since come round to Ulbricht's view, and Suslov's reminder of his change of attitude upset him. He was suddenly taken ill; the meeting was interrupted as he stalked out and went to bed in his train.

With Breshnev away, Pyotr Shelest, the Ukrainian Party's First Secretary, and Aleksadr Shelepin, the former Secret Police chief and leader of Russia's 'Young Turks', attacked and abused the Czechoslovak delegation. The main theme of the torrent of abuse was that 'Imperialist agents had wormed their way into the Czechoslovak Party's Praesidium'.

'If you really believe that there are Imperialist agents among the leaders of the Czechoslovak Communist Party', Mr Dubcek told the Russians calmly, 'then there is no point in continuing these talks.' And with that he in turn left the club-house where the talks were taking place.

In their train the Czechoslovak delegation considered returning to Prague. Then a group of five Russians came to their carriage and invited them to join the Soviet delegation for luncheon. It was the first time the two delegations had eaten together. After this first human contact the atmosphere became somewhat lighter; then, that night, miraculously cured of his ailment, Mr Breshnev returned to the talks.

During the day three letters had been delivered to Mr Breshnev in his train. One was from President Tito of Yugoslavia, the second from Signor Luigi Longo, the Italian Communist Party leader, and the third from M. Waldeck Rochet, the French Party's First Secretary. The message of the letters was identical: That Moscow could count on no support from any major Communist Party outside the Warsaw Pact countries, especially in its endeavour to hold a World Communist Conference in Moscow in November 1968, if it continued in its efforts to force Czechoslovakia into submission. It was perhaps this last-minute counter-attack rather than the Czechoslovaks' coolness which brought a sense of reality to the Soviet leaders. On Thursday morning the Czechoslovaks were pleasantly surprised to learn that the Politburo of the Soviet Communist Party was, after all, willing to let them follow their own democratic road to socialism. The price was stiff but not unacceptable.

A joint communique was issued, and spoke of 'a broad comradely exchange of opinion, held in an atmosphere of complete frankness, sincerity and mutual understanding'. The only hard fact to emerge was that the outcome of the Cierna talks should be a further meeting at Bratislava a few days later with the five signatories of the Warsaw Letter joining in. That the *modus vivendi* hammered out in Cierna must have contained a good measure of compromise for both sides was evident enough, but the extent of concessions the Czechoslovak leaders had to make on matters involving foreign policy, economic reform and the stationing of Soviet troops was far from clear in Czechoslovakia.

A nervous and impatient crowd gathered in the old town square in Prague that evening chanting 'Tell us the truth' and 'We want freedom'. Mr Smrkovsky, the Speaker of the National Assembly and one of the participants of the talks, appeared at a balcony to address the crowd. 'We defended our way of socialism and we were successful', he said in an improvised speech to a cheering crowd. 'We return with honour.' He said that the Czechoslovak delegation had gone to Cierna with two mandates—to defend Czechoslovakia's road to socialism and to prevent a breach with the other socialist countries. The Bratislava negotiations would be about economic and other forms of co-operation; polemics were now finished, the Warsaw Letter was forgotten. Many of his listeners remained sceptical, but Smrkovsky succeeded in persuading them to wait until the Bratislava meeting before passing judgment.

That evening President Svoboda addressed the nation. He spoke, he said, on behalf of the Party's Central Committee, Comrade Dubcek, and himself. His speech was not a success. Although he reassured the people that the path chosen by the party's January plenum would not be abandoned, at the same time he warned that the liberalization programme could only be carried out if Czechoslovakia remained a firm part of the social-ist commonwealth and relied on the support and co-operation of the Soviet Union. Exhausted after the gruelling pressure, he ended abruptly by appealing to all Czechoslovaks 'to support the results of our talks'.

But the millions of listeners wanted more than that: in the emotionally overcharged atmosphere of Prague, the lack of real information was enough to provoke demonstrations.

The Russians, also, said little about the outcome of the talks, although the silence about the specific demands of the Warsaw Letter and the sudden change of tone about Czechoslovakia in the Soviet press must have indicated to any intelligent reader that the Kremlin had climbed down. But an agreement can only be carried out if it is known to the executors, and details of it began leaking out in Czechoslovakia, at local Party cell level; as the dust settled after the first day's confusion the outlines of the mutual concessions and gains became clearer.

On August 2, Dubcek appeared on television to tell the Czechoslovaks that they could be satisfied with the results of the Cierna talks: 'We maintained the promises which we have made. For the Czechoslovak people, there is no other route than the one opened in January 1968. The Soviet comrades let themselves be persuaded that we are ready to prove by our acts that we shall not leave the socialist route.'

Apart from closer co-operation with Comecon—the Soviet bloc economic community—and the Warsaw Pact, the Czechoslovaks gave assurances that they would restrict the press from attacking the Soviet Union or from discussing foreign policy matters too freely—provided that their socialist neighbours observed the same restraint. They also promised to support the World Communist Conference in Moscow in November.

The most significant of the concessions made by the Russians was the acceptance that the Czechoslovak Army was capable of defending the country's western frontiers with West Germany. 'I wish to emphasize that the Czechoslovak Army is a firm link in the Warsaw Pact and a sufficient guarantee for the protection of our borders,' Dubcek said, thus implying that there was no need either for Soviet troops on the West German–Czechoslovak border.

Realizing the effect of President Svoboda's omission and to dispel any lingering anxiety and uncertainty,

Dubcek spoke openly about the most important issue—sovereignty:

'As soon as my aircraft touched down today I was asked whether our sovereignty was threatened. I sincerely state that it is not. We need friendship and good relations with the Soviet Union in the very interest of our sovereignty and the development of the process of democratization. . . .

'I tell you sincerely: you can be completely satisfied with the results and the spirit of these conversations. We kept the promises we made you and we have returned with the same conviction with which we went to Cierna—that of pursuing without turning aside from the path on which the Czechoslovak Communist Party and our entire people set out after last January. There is no other possibility for our people.'

This was straight talk. Dubcek had stood firm at Cierna against the invasion threat. He had at least won time.

The Cierna agreement may have been acceptable to the Russians, but it did not please Mr Ulbricht or the Polish Party boss, Wadislau Gomulka. When Gomulka arrived at Bratislava for the arranged meeting he at once demanded to know why it was necessary to meet again when all that needed to be said had already been said in the Warsaw Letter. The meeting began just after 10 a.m. on Saturday, August 3, on the second floor of Bratislava's glass-walled trade union meeting hall on a hill overlooking the Danube. It lasted two hours. The hall was screened by police and guards, but this did not stop Breshnev from going for a walk along the Danube, where he was mobbed by news-hungry Slovaks. In the afternoon a solemn ceremony was enacted at Bratislava's highest point, the Russian war memorial. Dubcek marched alongside Breshnev for a wreath-laying ceremony in honour of Russian troops who died in the liberation of Slovakia. To a Slovak who called to him: 'How is it going, Dubcek; are we all right?' the Party leader replied in a theatrical aside, so that Ulbricht would not hear: 'Don't worry; we are home and dry'. Then in the town hall of the Slovak capital the leaders of the Soviet Union, Poland, Hungary, Bulgaria, East Germany and Czechoslovakia put their signatures to a declaration of intent described by Czechoslovak officials as 'much more than a communique'. The declaration gave the Czechoslovaks a free hand to continue their internal reforms and democratization process, while limiting their freedom of action in establishing wider contact with the West. Apart from these slight curtailments of freedom of action, on every point of substance the advantage of the bargain went to Czechoslovakia. Prague saw the Bratislava communique as a 'State funeral with full rites for the Warsaw Letter.'

The operative passages of the communique conceded the right of every fraternal party to solve the questions of further Socialist development in accordance with their specific national conditions. They also reaffirmed the principles of equality, respect for sovereignty, national independence and territorial integrity—fully vindicating the political line of the Czechoslovak leaders and indicting the conduct of the Russians and their hard-line allies.

There were huge smiles, bear hugs and warm handshakes on the platform of the railway station at Bratislava. The men from the Kremlin had never been given such a grilling by the press before, but in the new spirit of relief and happiness that was enveloping the evening air they did not seem to mind the experience. Had the talks been a success, perhaps even a great success, asked a journalist? Mr Kosygin and Mr Breshnev beamed their assent, and there were more kisses all round. Breshnev, known to be one of the hard-liners inside the Kremlin who had favoured early military intervention, embraced not only Svoboda, whom he had known since their wartime campaigns on the Ukrainian front, but also Dubcek and other Slovak liberals. Breshnev had also fought in Slovakia. Now he clasped their hands and raised their arms together for the photographers, and told a television reporter amiably how much he liked Bratislava and how pleased he was at the successful outcome of the talks.

Smrkovsky, who had been imprisoned under the regime of Stalin, embraced with special warmth Mikhail Suslov, the lean, greying Soviet ideologist. Later asked why, the always candid and frank Smrkovsky said it was because Suslov had been so helpful, and had contributed so much towards the reconciliation. A surging crowd of 20,000 chanted 'Dubcek ... Dubcek', as Smrkovsky told them: 'Normal life resumes as from tomorrow. Everything is normal.'

More cautious Czechoslovak officials saw the outcome of the Cierna and Bratislava talks in a less optimistic light. The Russians, they argued, had not given up their designs, but had simply postponed the main decision. What they could not win with threats and menaces they now hoped to get through economic 'co-operation'. The Russians could expect with every reason that the difficult economic task Dubcek and Dr Sik had set for the nation would, in the short run, work for them. After all, the meaning of the Bratislava declaration was to tie Czechoslovakia's hands in foreign economic policy, denying Western trade, know-how and badly needed hard currency loans for modern machinery. In these conditions how could the economic miracle which Czechoslovakia needed be brought about?

But if words and official statements meant anything, Dubcek had undoubtedly won the second round of his fight to free Czechoslovakia from the shackles of Soviet-style Communism and give the Czechs and Slovaks a measure of freedom and democracy.

3 THE QUISLINGS' FAILURE

The key to the events on and before August 21 was the doublecross that failed, the attempt by a small clique of relatively unimportant C.C.P. functionaries to set up a Quisling regime. This was why the Russians, when they arrived, carried only three days iron rations and were forced to drink rainwater; and, as was seen near Pilsen, had to hunt squirrels with their tommy-guns and fry them over a fire for lack of something to eat.

The first clue in tracing the attempted doublecross was an apparently chance incident on August 15, nearly a week before the invasion. On the afternoon of that day the secretary of the C.C.P.'s Central Committee, Mr Alois Indra, sent his staff home early. When a girl secretary who had forgotten her lipstick returned to the office to look for it, she discovered Indra sitting at the teleprinter putting over a message. She was ordered out of the room by Indra, who was apparently furious that she had discovered him at the Telex, but she had seen enough of his message to be able to inform the Ministry of the Interior that Indra had been in touch with the Soviet Ambassador.

The next clue can be found on the night of August 20 when Karol Hoffmann, the former Minister of Culture under the Novotny regime, who had been appointed by Dubcek to the 'safe' and innocuous job of Director of the Office for Control and Administration of Means of Communication, issued orders that the main transmitting station of Prague Radio at Chesky Brod, was to stop all transmission during that night. (This order was countermanded early on the following morning after a radio announcer had seen the Russian tanks arriving in the city and had telephoned Smrkovsky, who was in bed, to tell him the invasion had started; Smrkovsky dressed and went to the Central Committee building after alerting the radio technicians and broadcasters, and Prague Radio went back on the air at 4.30 a.m.)

Earlier, at midnight, the Director-General of the Czechoslovak News Agency, Sulek, had arrived at his office and ordered the teleprinter staff to transmit world-wide a statement announcing that a 'revolutionary Government of workers and peasants' had assumed power and had invited the Russians to join in crushing the counter-revolution. Sulek was forcibly prevented by his colleagues and subordinates from personally Telexing this message to the world. Sulek thereupon left the C.T.K. building and a few days later it was announced by the Czechoslovak Government that he had been relieved of his post. Instead of his announcement, C.T.K. proceeded to broadcast news of the invasion and appeals to the outside world for help.

Early in the morning of August 21, when the tanks rolled in, President Svoboda, still in his pyjamas, watched from his window in Hradcany Palace as the Russians disarmed the palace guard outside. Soon afterwards two visitors were announced. One was the last Prime Minister of the Novotny era, Lenart, and the other was Indra. Wearing a dressing-gown over his pyjamas, Svoboda received them at his presidential desk, but kept them standing. Lenart and Indra presented for his signature a list of the members of a 'provisional Government of workers and peasants'. Indra, the former Minister of Transport, was to be Prime Minister, Karol Hoffman was to get his old job as Minister of Culture back and have control of press, radio, and television. Other Ministers on the list were Pavlovsky, the Old Guard Communist functionary and formerly Novotny's Ambassador in Moscow, who was to be Deputy Premier and Minister of Foreign Trade. The key post of Minister of the Interior, controlling the police and security forces, was to be given to the Deputy Minister of Education in the Cernik Government,

Chnoupek, a Slovak who was Moscow correspondent of a Bratislava newspaper for some years.

Svoboda's reaction to the demand that he should put his name to the new 'Government' was one word: 'Ven!' ('Get out!'). He repeated it several times with increasing emphasis, finally bawling it in tones which he had probably not used since he was a sergeant-major in the Czechoslovak Army in World War II.

At 9.30 a.m., Cernik, the Prime Minister, was arrested in his seat of office and led off handcuffed. His arrest was carried out in the name of the 'workers and peasants Government' of 'Prime Minister Indra'.

Alexander Dubcek was first told that foreign troops had violated his country's borders very late on August 20. At first he was unwilling to believe that a full-scale invasion was in progress. The reports he was getting were vague and inconclusive. Warsaw Pact manœuvres were still going on and the troop movements could have been no more than that. Or they could be a provocation, an attempt to make the 'counter-revolutionary forces' come out into the open and fight. This would provide an excuse for a real invasion. But Dubcek had reached agreement with the Soviet Union only a few days before and he could not imagine that the men he had come to terms with were now attacking him.

He was still giving the Russians the benefit of the doubt when a Soviet Embassy car drove into the square below his window at the Central Committee building on the embankment of the Vltava followed by a number of armoured cars. Kalmyks in Soviet Army uniform and K.G.B. security men in civilian clothes leapt out of the cars. A Czech in the square shouted at the invaders, abusing them; there was a burst of machine-gun fire and Dubcek and his colleagues saw the man fall dead. Only then did Dubcek realize what was happening to his country. He picked up one of the telephones to ring the Soviet Ambassador, Mr S. V. Cervonenko, saying as he did so: 'How can they do this to me? I have devoted my whole life to co-operation with the Soviet Union. This is my profound personal tragedy.'

He did not get through. A few seconds after he picked up the telephone the Kalmyks burst into the Central Committee room where the leaders were sitting. They ripped the telephone cord out of the wall. One of them cut the cord that lead round the wall, putting out of action all the telephones in the room. The Czechoslovak leaders, including Dubcek, Smrkovsky and Kriegel, were stood facing the wall with their hands up.

Also in the room was a friend of Dubcek's called Gahdos. The two men had known each other from childhood and for some years Gahdos had been Dubcek's chauffeur in Bratislava. When Dubcek became First Secretary in January 1968, he had to live in Prague, and there was already a chauffeur assigned who went with the job. So he took Gahdos on to his staff as a sort of personal bodyguard or valet. As Dubcek and his colleagues were being searched and manhandled against the wall, Gahdos suddenly flung himself on the officer in command. It was a brave but futile gesture. The officer merely drew his revolver and shot him. Before Gahdos died he made a statement to the Czechs who were looking after him. This has been typed and is being kept as one of the many historical records of the invasion.

As the politicians were being led out of the committee room, Smrkovsky stopped for a moment, stretched out his hand and took a handful of lump sugar from a bowl that was on the table. Smrkovsky has been in Russian prisons before and he knew that they never give sugar with tea. 'This will come in very useful,' he said as he stuffed the sugar into his jacket pocket.

Dubcek, Smrkovsky and Kriegel were taken down the stairs. Behind each man walked a soldier pinioning his arms. The K.G.B. men in civilian clothes were in charge of the operation, and there is a report that one of them stopped the party as they reached the foot of the stairs, produced a hypodermic and injected one of Dubcek's pinioned arms. At any rate, Czechs who saw Dubcek emerge from the Central Committee building say that he was bleary, staggering and half-unconscious.

The three men were driven away in armoured cars. On the way, ropes were tied round their necks, their bodies bent backwards, their feet and hands lashed together near the small of their backs and then joined to the neck-rope. They were thus in a constantly strained, backward-bending position, unable to struggle without putting pressure on their necks and possibly strangling themselves. Two of Dubcek's ribs were badly bruised; at first he feared they were broken.

All the arrested Czechoslovak Party leaders except Cernik were taken separately across the border in Russian tanks and armoured-cars, first to Warsaw, then to the Hungarian–Soviet border town of Munkacz. They finally met up in a mountain resort in the Carpatho-Ukraine, where they were joined by Cernik, who had been brought by plane. Their guards kept them under close observation day and night, awaiting the word from Prague that the 'workers and peasants Government' had assumed office, in which case they were to have been executed on the spot, as was Imre Nagy after the Hungarian uprising in 1956 just as soon as Kadar's Quisling Government had been formed.

But the 'workers and peasants Government' never got going, although, on August 22, its setting up was announced. Its leaders were the three pro-Russian members of the Czech Praesidium—Kolder, Bilak and of course Indra. But the announcement was treated with scorn by the Czechoslovaks, for during Wednesday night and early Thursday morning hundreds of delegates to the Fourteenth Party Congress—the one that the Russian invasion had been timed to prevent—had been secretly converging on Prague from all over the country.

The congress—originally scheduled for September 9, but now brought forward—was held secretly in a Prague suburb. It began in the early hours of Thursday with 936 delegates present. By midday more than a thousand of the 1,400 delegates originally chosen for the September 9 Congress were present. The Congress unanimously passed a resolution calling for the withdrawal of invading troops and the release of detained Czech leaders. It threatened a one-hour protest strike. It also elected a new 160-member Central Committee.

The fact that the meeting was held at all is a miracle. The delegates were summoned by clandestine radio and met in the Tesla electronics factory in Vysocany. The Russians arrested two-thirds of the Slovak delegates as they passed through the Prague Central railway station and have since argued that the Congress was, in consequence, illegal. The still free delegates arrived in small groups, on foot, and the meeting took place in the conference room of the factory. The Congress was under the chairmanship of Martin Vaculik, Chairman of the Praesidium, who ordered that there was not to be any applause or cheering and that any vote would be taken by a silent raising of hands. Their work hastily completed, the delegates left the way they had come, in small groups, on foot. The Russians, presumably acting on a tip-off, arrived at the factory two hours later, but the birds had flown.

4 RESISTANCE

A young girl tears up a cobblestone and hurls it at the invaders' oncoming tank. The stone clangs against the massive armour plating and clatters to the ground. The tank grinds on. If one were seeking an image to convey utterly futile defiance one could not find a better. And yet acts like this by the ordinary people of Czechoslovakia in those first few days after the invasion, multiplied hundreds of times across the nation and—of vital importance—made known to the outside world, took on a far more powerful significance. What they did could not stop the tanks and yet collectively these acts served to arouse indignation throughout the world against the invasion of a tiny country.

Certainly these acts of spontaneous defiance baffled the occupation troops whose conception of their mission—until then—must have been based purely on the line put out by the Kremlin—that the troops had been 'invited' into Czechoslovakia by the country's 'authorities' to protect it from a 'foreign-inspired counter-revolution'.

From the start, as an estimated 175,000 troops from Russia and her allies moved across Czechoslovakia's borders, it was painfully clear that any form of military resistance was utterly out of the question. The Czech Army is made up of an estimated 170,000 men— mainly national servicemen. So within hours the Kremlin had been able to move in more troops than the Czechs had. And this was merely the tip of the Soviet Union's daunting military iceberg. It is estimated that she had something like 140 divisions under arms compared with Czechoslovakia's 14. What is more, the Czech Army has for the last twenty years or more been deployed to face a possible invasion from the West and its Intelligence service is inextricably intertwined with Moscow's own. In other words, the Czech forces were not, and never had been, organized to face a possible invasion across the borders it shares with its Warsaw Pact allies.

By dawn on Wednesday, August 21, Soviet tank

crews had manned key points in Prague, and reinforcements were still sweeping into the helpless country. By that same Wednesday evening, all Czechoslovakia's major cities were held in a similar iron grip. By the next day the invaders had made their presence known on the country's farthest borders and had taken over control of most border checkpoints. Czech military sources estimated that at its peak in late August the invading force was around 650,000 strong—almost 100,000 more than the number of troops America had at that time stationed in Vietnam—and backed up by an unknown force of combat reserve units in the areas of the Soviet Union and her allies that surround Czechoslovakia.

It is only within the context of such overwhelming odds that the courage and the resilience of the Czech people can be appreciated fully. The resistance took many forms, ranging from the spontaneous stone throwing and taunting of Russian tank crews in the streets of Prague, through the cunning of the clandestine radio stations to the backs-to-the-wall defiance of the Czech leaders. And each form of resistance, however ineffective it might have been alone, served to strengthen the other manifestations. The people in the streets drew strength from their leaders, the leaders drew strength from the loyalty and courage in the streets.

While the Czechoslovak people were expressing their defiance to the invaders, their leaders were resisting with equal courage. President Svoboda was in Hradcany Palace which—like other government buildings—was ringed by tanks. Yet by some means—perhaps by tape recordings smuggled out of the castle—a defiant message from the President was broadcast to the Czech people on the evening of that first full day of the invasion.

The broadcast was heard at 9 p.m. London time (4 p.m. in New York). 'All day,' said Svoboda, 'I have done my utmost. I convened the Praesidium of the

44

National Assembly. I spoke with the members of the Government who are now, I hope, meeting Mr Cernik.' He called for the withdrawal of invasion troops but warned citizens to avoid acts of violence 'which might lead to irreparable consequences.' Yet he reassured his countrymen: 'There is no question of our turning back. The programme of the Communist Party and of the Government expressed the vital interests of the Czechoslovak people. Do not lose faith. We must remain united in our struggle for a better life for our country.'

The Czech Army leaders spoke out. A statement issued by the High Command, and signed by General Dzar, the Defence Minister, said that Czech troops would take orders only from President Svoboda.

In most situations these statements, promises, resolutions and ultimatums from a country's leaders might be dismissed as just so many words. But in Czechoslovakia in August 1968 they represented an essential bond between leaders and people, a bond which sustained the resistance of both groups.

A third element in the resistance was the condemnation of the Soviet action by the outside world. In many cases this was predictable. Criticism by Western Governments for instance was unlikely to surprise the Russians or affect the Kremlin policy, especially as there was never any suggestion of direct intervention. Nor would the criticism by fellow Communist countries like Rumania, Yugoslavia and Red China have much influence. But what must have surprised the Kremlin leaders—and perhaps made them rule out a more bloody crushing of the Czech liberalization movement —were the angry outbursts from the strong Western Communist parties in Italy and France, and perhaps most surprising of all the critical reaction of some sections of the East German population. Several factories in East Berlin were reported to have held protest rallies where several workers spoke of their shame that East German troops were involved in the invasion.

For days, with reckless impudence, in tiny hamlets as well as in the major cities—the taunting, jeering, whistling and scattered outbursts of violence against the occupation forces went on, despite pleas for caution from Czech leaders.

Russian tanks were daubed with swastikas (often as they waited for the traffic lights to change) and bombarded with bags of flour. One youth rammed a pole bearing the Czech flag down the muzzle of one tank's gun, others clambered aboard the machines and obscured the gunsights with chalk.

Reporters on the spot filed stories of incredible defiance. From Prague, Heinz Schewe of the *Observer* described two remarkable acts:

In one incident a young girl crawled under the fixed bayonets of a tank crew, chalked a swastika on the armour plating, spat, then crawled back out beneath the bayonets again. In another, a column of tanks was surging down Na Prikope Street as hundreds of jeering Prague citizens stood by, waving their fists. Suddenly, a cripple started his wheelchair bumping down the pavement towards the leading tank. Only yards from it a spectator dashed out to snatch up the man as another pulled the wheelchair clear. The cripple was shouting: 'I lost my legs in the war against Fascism. Now these Fascists from Moscow can finish the job and crush me to death!'

Sometimes the resistance took a more violent form than harsh words and slogans. Some of the most bitter fighting took place outside the Prague Radio building. Crowds of young Czechs gathered there from the early hours of Wednesday as the tanks closed in. Buses and trams were hauled across the front of the building to act as a barricade against the tanks. With flaming rags, Molotov cocktails and blazing newspapers the demonstrators tried to set fire to the invaders' trucks and tanks. Sometimes they succeeded. A couple of tanks went up in flames and an ammunition lorry was exploded.

Youths brandishing Czechoslovak flags flung themselves at the tanks, stuffing empty tin cans down the mouths of the guns, scrawling black swastikas on the green paintwork, and yelling 'Dirty Fascists go home', and 'At least Hitler had manners; he declared war before he invaded.' Others stood back hurling anything they could lay their hands on at the Soviet troops. Strips of torn upholstery, bits of broken furniture, beer crates, branches from fallen trees, accessories stripped from cars were all flung across the streets. Shirts were soaked in petrol, and dropped on the tanks, setting some of them ablaze and their crews scrambling off to safety. Signs were daubed on the bullet-pocked buildings: 'Asians go home. Tartars go home, Barbarians go home.'

Eventually the tanks rolled through the barricades and the radio station building was occupied. But it was fitting that this tense fighting should have happened here—for if any one thing helped to cement the Czechs together in defiance at this terrible time it was the radio stations, as we shall see later on.

Wenceslas Square was another focal point. In those first few days thousands of people jammed the square—watched over by surly Soviet tank crews sitting in their turrets. It was here that the leaflets and pamphlets produced by the underground Press were circulated freely and here too that the token one-hour national strikes—which occurred on the Thursday and Friday—were most visibly effective. Sirens would wail and car horns sound at midday to signal the start of the strike, and immediately all traffic would come to a standstill.

Similar events were happening all over the country; —even small villages where there was less mass hysteria were no less firm in their rejection of the invaders.

In one village on the river Upa the villagers stood in a

human chain across the bridge to block a Russian convoy which included tanks. The villagers held fast from 6.30 a.m. until 3 p.m., at which point the Russians turned back.

The spontaneous resistance movement among the people produced methods of annoying and delaying the invaders. The story that is told of the Russian freight train—engine number 5599—is a typical example. On the Friday morning, a clandestine radio station from Olomouc, in north-central Czechoslovakia, discovered that the train, heavily laden with radio- and television-tracking equipment, was on its way to Prague. The purpose of the equipment was obvious—to track down and silence the ubiquitous radio stations that were causing the invaders so much trouble. The Olomouc station's broadcast began: 'We have a report which will concern mainly railwaymen.' It then told them about the train. 'It stands to reason,' said the announcer, 'that the longer the train takes the better.' As the day wore on the station's appeals became more and more urgent—'Railwaymen and all of you who are listening—stop that train.'

And apparently the appeals were successful. It never did become clear how it had been done—but later that day the radio station announced that the train was stuck at Kraslikov—less than twenty miles from its departure point. The broadcast concluded: 'Comrades, railwaymen, we thank you.'

It was in Bratislava that there was the most physical resistance to the occupying Red Army. Several tanks were set on fire by puncturing the petrol tanks. Ordinary farm pitchforks were laid in the tanks' paths in such a way that the upward pointing prongs were caught in the caterpillar tracks; and many tanks were brought crunching to a halt by this primitive method. But later on 'passive resistance' turned out to be even more effective. One afternoon, a number of tanks were stand-

48

ing in a park in Bratislava, their crews armed and their guns at the ready. The young Slovaks who were 'passively' outstaring the Russian soldiers decided that they did not care to be watched over in this way, and so a group of them set out and collected from all over the city a mass of pictorial pornography and photographs of nudes torn out of Western periodicals that lately had become available. They then took the pictures in cardboard boxes into the park, and offered them to the Russian troops as presents. Some of the soldiers, far away from home and from wives or girl friends, still suffering from the shock of their hostile reception, accepted pictures gratefully. Others retained their dignity and refused the presents, and then the young Slovaks would hold the pictures up in the air so that the young Russians could not avoid seeing them. It was some time before the Russian commander realized what was happening. Deciding that the efficiency and vigilance of his men was being gravely impaired, he gave the order for the hatches of the tanks to be closed and for watch to be kept through machinegun slits and the periscopes. As the soldiers disappeared from view and silence reigned over the park, the Slovaks took coarse delight in declaring that the Red Army soldiers, having been abused for days by the local population, were now doubtless abusing themselves.

But that was not all. To complete their 'passive resistance', the daring young Slovaks then clambered on to the tanks and stuck brown sticky paper over the periscopes, rendering the crews, for a minute or two, totally blind and quite helpless.

What happened when Colonel Kovalyov's advance force took over the Bratislava 'hrad', an old castle at the town's high point, was even more interesting. After his troops had settled in, he was approached courteously by one of the senior officials of the museum. Would it be possible, the official asked, to go into the museum and check that the important historical treasures were still there. The colonel agreed readily—presumably deciding that it was important for him to be seen as a protector of Slavic culture. He sent for a lieutenant, who let the curator in. The museum official looked round his exhibits and found, to his relief, that they were intact.

Then finding that the lieutenant had left him, the museum curator went down into the cellars of the museum and turned off the main water supply. He then left the museum, thanking the Russian troops for their kindness. It was not until later that the Colonel's staff discovered they no longer had any fresh water, and when they were ordered to find some elsewhere, they discovered that throughout Bratislava supplies had somehow been cut off. The problem of water became a serious one for the occupying forces, and for some days drinking water for the Colonel and his senior officers had to be ferried from Hungary by helicopter. For the troops, things were not so good. The slogan 'not even a drop of water for the occupiers' was rigidly followed by the Slovaks.

The tank crews needed it more than most, because they were living off 'concentrate', a kind of powder which is highly nutritious but very unpalatable. It needs to be mixed up with some liquid, but whenever a soldier stepped gingerly down from his tank to fill a jerrican of water from a tap, a group of Slovaks would gather quickly round, and warn him sympathetically that they would advise him not to drink the water because it had been poisoned by the 'counter-revolutionaries.' 'All right to wash in, but not to clean the teeth', they smiled. This was more than enough to put the soldiers off taking even one sip of the water, and they would scramble back into their tanks and wonder when they would ever encounter their 'Czechoslovak friends', of whom they had been told only the week before.

The troops ended up by scooping water from roadside puddles or by lowering buckets into the Danube. The former proved often to be safer, because the Blue Danube in Bratislava is particularly murky, polluted as it is with oil from the nearby refineries. The result of this was that many of the soldiers fell ill with gastric complaints, and—deprived also of proper food, sleep and sanitary facilities—became very debilitated.

By this time all the occupying troops knew they were not welcome. The evidence was there for them to see wherever they went in the slogans plastered over the walls. Slogans included the appeal to the emotions—'Russian soldier! How will you be able to tell your mother you have been killing children?'; the facetious —'Why bother to occupy our State Bank? You know there is nothing in it'; and the fable approach: 'An elephant cannot swallow a hedgehog'.

* * *

The first reports of the Russian–Warsaw Pact invasion initiated weeks of frenzied activity by the world's press, both East and West: this was clearly one of the most important news stories of the decade, opening up gloomy prospects of a dramatic turn for the worse in Great Power relationships, perhaps even war.

Murray Sayle was on the first plane from London to Vienna on Wednesday, August 21. He writes:

I rented a car at Vienna airport and drove to the smallest border crossing I could find on the map, at a place called Znojmo. I bought two 20-litre jerricans of petrol and drove towards the customs barrier. There were crowds of people anxiously interrogating everyone who came out.

The Czech border police seemed surprised that I was trying to get into and not out of Czechoslovakia, but after a brief questioning they issued me with a visa. As I motored towards Prague I met tourists driving at speed the other way. Many had large home-made flags on their cars and such signs as 'Italy–neutral' stuck to their windscreens.

Twenty kilometres from the border I met the Russians. A convoy of six armoured-cars and two heavy lorries, towing howitzers, was stationary at a crossroads. They had plenty of ammunition and the troops were in full combat gear. They clearly meant business, but they were lost. The signposts had been removed, and in the classical pose of a bewildered motorist in a strange country, the commander of the column was studying a map. A trooper with a sub-machine-gun pulled me up. I shouted 'Tourist!' After a cursory glance at my Austrian number-plate he waved me on.

The first substantial town I came to was Havlickuv Brod. In the main square people were pushing farm carts into position to block the road and others were daubing up the signs with which I was soon to become familiar. They were in all the languages of the invading Warsaw Pact powers. I noted some down: 'Soldaten, warum sind sie bei uns?' 'Soldiers, why are you among us?', 'Russians go home', 'Polish soldiers and Comrades, do not fire on our children' and 'Not a drop of water for the occupiers'. My initial impression, which did not change in the weeks that followed, was one of unity, defiance—and fear.

I decided to take a chance and approached a police officer in uniform. Like many Czechs in responsible jobs he spoke some German. I explained to him that I was not a tourist, but a British journalist trying to get to Prague to cover the invasion. I told him that it was in the interests of the Czechs that the rest of the world should have as much reliable information as possible about what was going on in their country. He readily agreed and said: 'Give me twenty minutes.' I used the time to drive to the Havlickuv Brod airport, having been told that the Poles were beginning to land there.

Sure enough there was a Polish light aircraft and a group of air force men setting up a radio. The Czech flag at the airport was at half-mast. I decided it was prudent not to try to interview the Poles and returned to Havlickuv Brod.

By this time the police officer was back with a colleague in civilian clothes. 'This man will show you the way up to Prague by the side roads,' he said. 'The main road is hopeless. We expect the Russians to come down it at any minute. Good luck.'

My policeman guide and I drove on a complicated route of farm tracks and country lanes. At one point we forded a shallow stream. We saw no Russians at all and were pulled up only once at an improvised road-block manned by Czech youths, one of whom had a pistol—the only Czech civilian I saw with a weapon during the whole of my time in Czechoslovakia. My guide explained the situation and they waved us on.

On the outskirts of Prague at first light there were extraordinary traffic jams as motorists, mostly foreign tourists, tried to get out of the city. At one garage which was still selling petrol there was a queue of some hundred French cars led by a French Military Attaché with the improbable name of Captain Marmalade. They were trying to get petrol to drive to the border, but supplies were low and soon ran out.

As we drove through the Prague suburbs we saw staggering numbers of Russian tanks and armoured-cars deploying through the city. I had expected a score or so tanks, but at the peak of the build-up there were five hundred in Prague, cordoning the railway station, airport, radio station, television headquarters, and holding the bridges and crossroads throughout the city.

Wenceslas Square in the heart of the city was littered with wreckage from the wild shooting of the night before and the front of the Bohemian National Museum, a huge building which dominates the Place, was covered

With bullet and shrapnel scars. Most of the windows had been shot out.

In a side street the Russians were towing away a burnt-out tank. It was clear that the civil administration in the city had either broken down completely or had deliberately ceased to function. The Czech police certainly refused to co-operate with the Russians and stood smoking while people painted up slogans; 'United States in Vietnam, Soviet Union in Czechoslovakia', 'Wake up Lenin, Breshnev has gone mad'—one of the most popular slogans of the whole occupation—and even the ringing defiance of the Spanish Civil War: 'No pasaran', 'They shall not pass'.

The Russians were busy raiding the offices of the radio and television services and newspapers, and occupying them. They 'searched' the offices of the Writers' Union—with crowbars—claiming that they were looking for subversive literature, and in the process wrecked the place.

But although they had arrived with three military bands among their extensive equipment for pacification, the Russians had no policemen, no Czech experts, and no way of enforcing their rule. Clandestine newspapers were in profusion, coming out under the noses of the Russians—several newspapers were printed in the government lithograph office not fifty yards from a Russian tank emplacement. Prague was alive with rumours that large numbers of agents from the K.G.B. had arrived to conduct a mass purge, and that hundreds of people were being arrested and deported. The truth was quite different. There was a bitter tussle between the Russians and the S.T.B., the Czech Secret Police, for possession of the S.T.B. building and its copious files, and it was not until Saturday that the Russians got possession of the building, only to discover that the files with their invaluable lists of names and addresses had been taken away.

It was during this conflict that fifteen S.T.B. men mysteriously disappeared. The Czechs say that the Russians had arrested them and they have been demanding them back ever since; the Russians say they have not got them. The Russians are known to have expected that they would get much more from the S.T.B. than the total non-co-operation which they found. What has happened to the missing fifteen remains a mystery.

Day after day, the anti-occupation posters and pamphlets became ever more strident; on Friday a youth handed me a cyclostyled newspaper in English headed U.S.S.R. with the double S heavily underlined. A sign appeared on the wall of the Prague Maternity Hospital 'Leonid [Breshnev], send 10 more tanks—20 more counter-revolutionaries arrived here today'. In an exceptional feat of resistance which throughout showed great technical skill, someone succeeded in erecting a neon sign reading 'DUBCEK—SVOBODA' on a building in Wenceslas Place. Some of the youths distributing the clandestine newspapers were shot dead by the Russians and the funerals attended by hundreds of people fed the fires of bitterness.

*   *   *

Perhaps the crucial role in the Czech resistance was played by the radio and television service. The Russians, with their passion for organization, have all along insisted that the clandestine radio and television were being operated by an underground organization, a well-prepared group of skilled and experienced counter-revolutionaries.

The truth is quite different. This aspect of the resistance was improvised; there was no secret organization and there was no counter-revolutionary master-mind directing it. What we were seeing, transmitted from Czechoslovakia and relayed all over the world, was an inventive people ingeniously exploiting the possibilities of modern communications, notably in the operation of the world's first clandestine television service.

The television studios concentrated on providing newscasts rather than direct news, which radio was able to do better because of its simpler technical facilities and the difficulties of processing cameramen's film. They concentrated on getting prominent politicians to appear before the cameras and on providing interpretative comment on the news to maintain public morale.

Russian attempts to close the television service down were frustrated from the start because not all the offices and studios were in the same place. Like the BBC's establishments in London, they were dotted all over Prague. The first Soviet troops entered one of the studios in Gorky Street only a few hours after the invasion started. They ordered the entire staff to disperse, but tried to persuade the director, Mr Pelikan, who was also a parliamentary deputy, to stay on and run the television station for them under the supervision of the security forces. He refused, and later was able to escape.

Wherever the Russians went to occupy a TV studio they took wirecutters with them; sometimes they severed wires without any clear idea of what they were doing—with disastrous and sometimes comical results. The group which took over the Gorky Street building cut a few wires and then settled down to sleep in a room on the ground floor, blissfully unaware that the transmitters were continuing to send out emergency news programmes. They had cut the wrong wires.

As the troops became more active in hunting down the TV men and their clandestine studios, the news department kept programmes on the air by moving from one emergency building to another. One such studio was in a cinema in the centre of Prague, others were in factories on the outskirts of the city. Factories were chosen because it became known that the Soviet troops had orders not to occupy them under any circumstances, so as not to antagonize the 'friendly workers'. Some of the transmissions were from the premises of firms who actually made TV and electronics equipment and thus had testing facilities which were easily adapted for transmission purposes. An additional technical facility which enabled the service to keep going was a scientific development invented by Czech electronic engineers two years before and still not in general use. It consists of a small TV box transmitter about five feet long and three feet wide. It can be worked by one operator, and those used by the Czechs included instant self-destroying devices which could be operated if the Russians found them. They were fed with speech impulses from microphones or even from someone speaking into a telephone twelve miles away, and the link was by what a Czech technician simplified into a 'sort of laser beam'.

Their advantage was that they could operate without any wire link between the speaker with the microphone and the transmitter. This meant that the Russians could not tap the transmission and discover the origin of the message; indeed, the worst that could happen was that the transmitter should be discovered. More often than not the transmitters were moved before they were found, but in the few cases when there was not time to do this they were destroyed at once by the built-in explosive charge. One of these ingenious devices was used during the secret Party Congress in the electronics factory; and eight journalists, readers and technicians ensured a non-stop output of news and comment which infuriated the Russians.

When Murray Sayle arrived in Prague during the evening of August 21 the clandestine television was just starting its broadcasts and he naturally watched it with interest:

The programmes were introduced by the star Czech television reporter, Jiri Kanturek, and the news was read by Kamila Mouskova, who has been the leading Czech newscaster since the service began ten years ago. To Czechs, these people are as familiar as Britain's David Frost or America's Huntley and Brinkley. The programmes appeared to be coming from a normal studio, with a background of Czech national flags and big pictures of Svoboda and Dubcek. The early programmes consisted of a procession of well-known Czechs, from every field of activity: sporting stars, intellectuals, and such irreproachable figures as the Professor of Veterinary Science at the University of Prague. Their message, in many different forms, was the same—a call to passive resistance and non-co-operation.

I was as mystified as any Czech as to where these broadcasts were coming from and wondered how, in a country occupied by a powerful army, they were getting away with it. Some days later Colonel Emil Zatopek, the Czech long-distance runner, let me into the secret. Zatopek, a national hero, continued a cheerful defiance throughout the occupation. He speaks a rapid if somewhat innaccurate English, and there is no doubt where he stands: 'We were getting the socialism going real nice here before these bloody Russians came.'

Zatopek, after removing the tabs of his rank to avoid compromising anyone, drove me to the Dum Hotel-oveho Bydleni apartment building on Na Petrinach Street in the suburb of Petriny, a half-finished block twelve storeys high. The 'studio' was a kitchen in a flat on the twelfth floor.

What had happened was this. As the Russian troops arrived to take over the television centre in the heart of Prague on the morning of August 21, there was confused scuffling outside, and the television workers were alerted by the tanks shelling the building next door.

An outside broadcast truck, normally used to cover football matches, was parked behind the centre. As the Russians entered through the front door, the producer Mirek Lang and reporter Jiri Kanturek, with a volunteer crew of technicians, commandeered the truck and drove it to a forest just outside Prague. They hid in the forest during the day and at dusk drove the truck to the half-finished block of flats on Na Petrinach Street. The television men, assisted by a group of Czechoslovak Army signals' technicians, arrived with rolls of brown paper and blacked out the uncompleted apartment on the twelfth floor. They set up their studio in the kitchen, and mounted the parabolic antenna from the outside broadcast truck on the roof, camouflaging it with Army blankets and some briars which the builders had left on the roof of the building after the 'topping out' ceremony (fortunately, Czech builders hoist quite a respectable-sized tree for this ancient rite). The antenna, with its cover of bushes and blankets, was beamed at the small village of Bukova, where the local television transmitter for Pilsen (where the beer comes from, 80 km from Prague) is situated. From Bukova the signal was retransmitted by a microwave link to local television stations throughout the country. The crew then drove the outside broadcast truck, stripped of its gear, to the other side of Prague, where they abandoned it, and by 10 p.m. on Wednesday, August 21 they were ready to go on the air with a message of defiance.

The Russians were then faced with the problem of trying to find how the signal was coming from Prague (if it *was* coming from Prague) and where it was being fed into the national television grid.

I studied the layout in the half-finished block of flats, and it was undetectable from the outside, although all week Russian armoured-cars were patrolling back and forth in the street outside. While the service operated, the television crews slept on the floor of the penthouse apartment, and were sent meals from a Czech military hospital three blocks away.

Meanwhile Zatopek, who is instantly recognized everywhere in Czechoslovakia, had been awakened by four Czechoslovak Army officers in the early hours of the 21st. 'Have you come to take me with you or to take me away?' asked Zatopek. One of the officers replied, 'Emil, the country needs your help.' Zatopek spent the next four nights sleeping in different houses in Prague. On the Friday night, August 23, an Army officer drove him to the kitchen television studio, now decorated with its pictures of Svoboda and Dubcek.

There he made his first underground broadcast, as one of the long list of Czech notables who by so appearing, established themselves in Russian eyes as determined counter-revolutionaries. By the second Sunday of the occupation the Russians were reduced to systematically visiting every television transmitter to find where the mystery broadcasts were coming from. Somehow they discovered that programmes were being relayed from Bukova, and they asked the staff at the Prague television headquarters where it was. There are three Bukovas in different parts of the country, and a large-scale map of Czechoslovakia is needed to find any one of them. According to Zatopek, the Czech television men offered the Russians the best they could, a village called Bukovany, several hundred kilometres away. A detachment of Russian armoured-cars raced to Bukovany, and the astonished inhabitants had to submit to a totally inexplicable Russian search for a non-existent transmitter.

The clandestine studio finally went off the air on the Sunday of the Moscow agreement. 'I am sure it was the television and radio which kept our people together,' said Zatopek. 'And as well, it was a hell of a lot of bloody fun.'

August 21st. A Soviet tank enters the centre of Prague (*Keystone*)
A girl rushes for cover as Russian tanks open fire (*United Press International*)

One of the Russian 'liberators' (*Keystone*)

Prague, August 21st. A Soviet tank in flames (*United Press International*)
Prague, August 21st. Students carry away a wounded comrade (*United Press International*)

The statue of Saint Wenceslas (*United Press International*)

Alexander Dubcek (*Keystone*)

President Ludvik Svoboda (*Keystone*)

Russian tanks in the streets of Pilsen (*Keystone*)

Prague, the morning of August 22nd. The barricades go up (*United Press International*)

August 22nd, the afternoon. A street scene in Prague (*Keystone*)

A sit-down demonstration in Wenceslas Square (*Keystone*)

An unsmiling President Svoboda acknowledges greetings as he drives to the fateful Kremlin meeting (*United Press International*)

The clandestine radios were less spectacular, technically, but they were just as important in stiffening Czechoslovak resistance. Some of the transmitting gear was removed from the studios before the Russians arrived, but the greater part was mobile transmitting equipment supplied by the Czech Army. Czechoslovakia is small enough for everyone to know everyone, and informal contacts between the radio people and Army officers in a similar line of work were easily arranged in a few hours. Together, they moved the mobile transmitters every few hours. They used the same wavelengths as the normal Czech broadcasting service and they called themselves by the same names: Radio Prague, Czechoslovakia One, North Bohemia, and so on. The announcers did not identify themselves by name, but their voices were well known to every Czech: there was no question of the authenticity of the programmes. Nobody appeared live for these broadcasts. All programmes were taped in places far away, and the tapes delivered by car or bicycle with the co-operation of bodies like the C.C.P., the Boy Scout movement (a new organization which dates from last January), the Army and volunteer groups of students.

Suggestions to the Czechoslovaks on how to set about 'passive resistance' and, generally, how not to co-operate with the invaders, were frequently broadcast. The work was actually carried out by listeners and many thousands, perhaps hundreds of thousands of people, were involved; but the directions themselves were improvised by the radio people as they went along. The universal success of the plan to make things difficult for the invaders came, not from the efficiency of an organization, but from Czech solidarity, from a rediscovered national pride. The radio gave a great opportunity for the realization of the creative energy which has characterized Czechoslovak intellectual life since January 1968. Poets and journalists had their work broadcast by the radio to an appreciative audience. New songs were composed especially for the occasion, and something of the heady atmosphere of the revolution of 1917 reappeared. I wonder how many British or American journalists in similar circumstances could come up with something as simple and effective as this song:

> *You have tanks,*
> *We have the truth,*
> *And our finest hour.*
> *You have only power*
> *To beat and betray,*
> *To beat and betray,*
> *I only sing a song,*
> *And this is what I say:*
> *Go away, go away!*

The Czechoslovaks were not the only people operating an 'underground' radio service in the early days of the occupation. On the first day something called 'Radio Vltava' came on the air. The Vltava is the river on which Prague stands, but there was nothing very Czech about these broadcasts. They came from the regular civil radio transmitter at Karl-Marx-Stadt, in East Germany, just over the Czech border, although they purported to be broadcast from Czech soil. The station's programmes were introduced by the sound of a gong playing the opening bars of a Russian pop tune called *Nights in Moscow*, and the staff appeared to consist of two people: a woman who spoke Slovak rather than Czech, and a male announcer who did his best in Czech with a heavy Russian accent for the first few days, but soon gave up and confined himself to broadcasting messages to the occupation troops in straight, excellent Russian.

The programmes of Radio Vltava consisted of news culled directly from *Tass* and *Pravda*, and human interest programmes which seem to have been improvised in a great hurry. One of these was the tearful reading by the lady with the Slovak accent of a letter from a Russian war widow, who at some unspecified time had visited Czechoslovakia to see the grave of her husband, killed fighting to liberate Czechoslovakia from the German invaders. The unnamed widow spoke feelingly of the Czechoslovak friends she had made during her visit and their rather irrelevant enthusiasm (in the circumstances) for the policies of the Soviet Union.

This form of propaganda did not go down very well with the Czechs and Radio Vltava, along with such related enterprises as the Russians' occupation newspaper *Zpravy*, outlived its usefulness and went off the air a week after the invasion began.

5 MEETING IN MOSCOW

The situation looked more and more hopeless as time wore on. Nobody knew what had happened to Dubcek, Cernik, or the other Czech leaders who had been arrested by the Russians. There were fears that they had been executed; there were certainly strong rumours of their liquidation by a firing squad. The country had ground to a halt because of an economically crippling general strike in protest against the invasion. The people were restive. They continued their passive resistance, but with increasing dissatisfaction and there was a danger of anarchy. The Soviet Union's attempts to find quislings to run a puppet regime had totally failed, and there seemed, to one man at least, the danger that if something were not done quickly to get the country going again, the Russians would step in and assume a full military dictatorship.

Through the long night of August 22 the white-haired, 72-year-old President of Czechoslovakia, Ludvik Svoboda, wondered what to do. Outright defiance of the invaders could not go on for ever. Perhaps the Russian leaders were by now ready to concede that they had made a blunder and would be prepared to discuss a leadership compromise between the new progressives and the conservatives backed by the Kremlin.

It is not yet clear whether Svoboda broached this idea with the Russians, or whether they contacted him, but at 7 a.m. on August 23 he had a conference at Hradcany Palace, his official residence, with the Soviet Ambassador, Mr S. V. Cervonenko. Cervonenko is thought to have been one of those who advised Moscow's leaders that in invading they could expect the support of the Czech working people, a colossal misjudgment. This time, however, Cervonenko was acting as peacemaker; he told Svoboda, a former Army general and 'Hero of the Soviet Union' that the Kremlin wanted him to go to Moscow provided that he took with him some of the hard-liners, including Mr Bilak and Mr Indra. Svoboda agreed, and announced his proposed trip himself through a dramatic radio broadcast:

'The following comrades will join me on this trip: Dr Husak, General Dzur, Comrades Piller, Bilak, Indra and Dr Kucera.

'I have informed the National Assembly of our republic about my trip. On this occasion I wish to address myself to all dear friends to thank you sincerely for all the support you have given me and for your confidence, and I beg you to continue to support my actions with your confidence. I urgently ask you to maintain prudence, to avoid any action or contacts that would exacerbate the atmosphere in our country and relations with the representatives of the foreign armies. . . . I assume that we shall return by tonight. Upon my return I shall inform the constitutional organs and you, all dear fellow citizens, on the results of my negotiations.'

As their plane climbed out of Prague, Svoboda and his colleagues weighed up their chances of success. They had made no headway with the Soviet military authorities but because of the support of the people and their coolness in defiance, there were still some cards left in their hands. The massive Soviet propaganda campaign claiming that all 'healthy' elements in Czechoslovakia welcomed the invasion as a move to save the Communist system from a right-wing *coup* had been a dismal flop. Despite Soviet claims of wide acceptance for the intervention, none of the Kremlin leaders had personally gone on record to associate themselves with the action, nor had they felt able to identify those Czech leaders who had requested the presence of the Russian troops. And, most important of all, the Soviet Union had not been able to name one political figure or group of men that might prove acceptable to the Czechs and the Slovaks.

The scene that awaited them at Moscow's Vnukovo Airport was almost unbelievable. Alongside the Russian red hammer and sickle fluttered the red, white and blue flag of Czechoslovakia. There were banners of welcome, and as Svoboda stepped down from the aircraft there was a 21-gun salute. And there to greet him, beaming as if they were meeting an old friend, were Communist Party chief Leonid Breshnev, Premier Alexei Kosygin, and President Nikolai Podgorny. It was the ruling Kremlin triumvirate's first public appearance in Moscow since the invasion. There were bear hugs and kisses; it was tragically reminiscent of the scene at Bratislava only a few weeks before, when the Kremlin reached and signed an agreement with Mr Dubcek.

After this ceremonial welcome, reserved only for distinguished guests, there was a motorcade procession into the city centre, with Svoboda and his three hosts standing together in the back of a black Zil convertible. Svoboda waved to the crowds lining the route, but he looked sad and tired. Breshnev continued to beam broadly and waved his hand vigorously; Podgorny, well suntanned, looked cheerful, but Kosygin appeared glum. The motorcade passed under more banners proclaiming: 'Long live the Soviet Union,' and 'Long live the Soviet–Czechoslovak friendship.' Along Lenin Prospect the people stood three or four deep, amid thousands of soldiers and policemen. Their cheers rippled with well-timed precision along the pavements, nicely ahead of the procession of black limousines. Many of the thousands of people had been given early release from their factories to greet President Svoboda, although not all of them knew what they were there for. One Western correspondent asked his neighbour in the crowd: 'Who are those men?' 'Kosygin, Breshnev and Podgorny,' came the reply. 'Yes, but who was the fourth man?' 'I don't know. Some foreigner, I suppose.'

The hosts and their guests drove straight to the Kremlin and began their talks immediately. Svoboda refused to negotiate unless Mr Dubcek was also present; talks were adjourned for the night, and Svoboda and his colleagues were given rooms in the Kremlin. A brief statement was issued by the Soviet news agency *Tass* describing the talks as being held in a 'frank and comradely atmosphere'. Those who are accustomed to reading between the lines on such statements read into this that there was already some tough bargaining.

The next morning the talks continued while the world watched, baffled. One newspaper published a story stating that Mr Dubcek was safely in Prague in the National Assembly building. Most papers reported that the Party Secretary had attended the Moscow talks, and was on his way home to his old job after securing a 'complete triumph'.

In fact, while many of the newspapers were declaring

Dubcek's day of triumph, he was inside the red walls of the Kremlin, fighting for his political, perhaps even his physical, life. He and Cernik had been driven to the Kremlin in the morning and allowed to join the talks between Svoboda and the Soviet leaders. By this time, Breshnev and Kosygin had probably convinced their colleagues that Dubcek would have to remain the Party boss in Czechoslovakia, at least for the time being. Certainly the bitter personal attacks on him in the Soviet press ended abruptly, and were replaced by repeated denunciations of the secret Communist Party Congress held in the Prague electronics factory, when support for Dubcek had been 1,094 votes to one.

Dubcek, Smrkovsky, Cernik and Kriegel were still tied when they were first brought into the presence of Leonid Breshnev and the Russian leaders in Moscow, but later they were set free. Breshnev read them a prepared statement, accusing them of harbouring counter-revolution, and repeating the spurious story of how Soviet forces had been 'invited' into Czechoslovakia. His diatribe lasted more than an hour. Breshnev was only just beginning to realize the extent of his misinformation. He had not reckoned on having to deal with these four men. By rights a new right-thinking government should already have been in existence. It should have been necessary merely to dispense with the four men's services, perhaps even with their lives. But Breshnev had failed to find an alternative regime and so was forced to bluster and improvise.

He had a number of ideas to 'propose' to the Czechs. His most helpful suggestion was that they adopt the 'Polish variant'. This is the term now used to describe the new-style Gomulkaism, regarded as a heresy twelve years ago by the Russian leaders but now recognized as the system most likely to keep their westernmost satellites obedient and reasonably content. The essential ingredients of this 'variant' are (1) a permanent Russian military presence on the satellite territory, (2) internal independence as far as is consistent with the general interest of the socialist bloc, (3) rigid control over the press and all means of communication, (4) strict supervision over the country's intellectuals, the ringleaders of all movement towards 'bourgeois liberalism' and 'social democracy'.

Breshnev told the four leaders that it was only with these safeguards that the Soviet Union could allow a measure of self-government in a dependent East European country. If they refused to accept and enforce the safeguards, the alternatives were drastic. The country would be split and part of it absorbed into the Soviet Union—an idea first mooted by Stalin in 1946. He told them the Soviet Union would do anything to defend herself and her system, even if it meant destroying the 14 million inhabitants of Czechoslovakia, that in the past fifty years the Soviet Union had killed many more than 14 million in its own defence, and was ready, if necessary, to do the same again. Czech and Slovak lands would be completely repopulated with Soviet citizens.

The Russian hand was so strong and was being played so ruthlessly that Dubcek and his colleagues were powerless. The only way out was suicide, although even this would have been hard to accomplish. According to Lord Bethell's sources, President Svoboda, who was physically at least a free man during the discussions, did at one point draw a revolver and threaten to kill himself. It was his only recourse, and it did have some effect on the Russians who have some respect for their old ally in the struggle against Fascism.

Then the Russian leaders acted just as they had done a few weeks earlier at the Cierna talks—they moderated their attitude and made it clear they were prepared to wear Dubcek for a while, although they could not accept his plans. They told him that Czechoslovakia would have to renounce all credits from capitalist countries, that censorship would have to be reimposed, followed by a thorough purge of foreign correspondents in Prague, that relations with Rumania and Yugoslavia would have to be cooled down, and that the new friendly relationship built up with West Germany would have to be replaced by hostility. And just to make sure that Dubcek had no illusions they returned him that night to where he had been in detention; a house outside Moscow. The hospitality of the Kremlin was not for him.

The next morning the Russian leaders conferred with other Soviet bloc leaders who had flown into Moscow— East Germany's Walter Ulbricht, Poland's Wadislaw Gomulka, Mr Kadar from Hungary and Mr Zhivkov from Bulgaria. What happened at that meeting is unknown, but the outcome appears to have been a toughening in the Russian attitude, with threats to Dubcek of liquidation if the Czechs failed to annul within ten days the decisions of the secret Party Congress.

Svoboda and his colleagues left the Kremlin late that night, to fly back to Prague. It must have been a comfort to have Dubcek and Cernik with him (Indra had been left behind, having had a heart attack). But he must have reflected, as his car sped silently and un-noticed to the airport in the middle of the night, that his departure from Moscow was not quite as auspicious as his arrival, and a bad omen for the future.

At the airport Svoboda realized that Dr Kriegel was absent, and still under detention. Labelled by Kosygin at the Cierna talks as a 'Jew from Galizia', Kriegel had been arrested at the same time as Dubcek, but was prevented from participating in the Moscow meeting. Svoboda refused to leave Moscow without him. When Kriegel finally rejoined his colleagues on the return journey, it was evident he had been tortured.

He was unable to speak or write coherently, and he did not regain his faculties for some days.

All the Czechoslovak leaders returned home physically, morally, and mentally exhausted.

6 THE VILLAGE

All the newspapers were publishing eye-witness accounts of the events in Prague, but what was happening in the villages? On Friday, August 30, I suggested to Murray Sayle in Prague that he should visit some small village in the countryside to see how people outside the big towns were getting along under the occupation. It took him more than two hours to drive thirty kilometres from Prague to a village of some 500 people, perched on a hilltop amid cornfields and orchards. This is what he found:

Driving in Czechoslovakia in the first days of the occupation was a nightmare for journalists and occupation forces alike. Every signpost had been obliterated, and almost every village either had no name at all, or had been fancifully and defiantly renamed. I passed five villages named 'Dubcek' and two railway stations called 'Svoboda'. At almost every crossroads there was an arrow painted on the asphalt and a daubed sign: 'MOCKBA [Moscow] 2,000 km.'

With all this, it took me quite a while to find my village. When I had it in view, I noticed one or two unusual features: it consisted entirely of new buildings, and it must be about the only village in the whole of Czechoslovakia without a village church.

As I drove up, I passed a lush field of oats and a company of young soldiers of the Czechoslovak National Army, stripped to the waist, getting the harvest in. Not far away, on a bare field, was a circle of Russian armoured cars. Their crews were busy with a noisy game of football. But there was no contact and certainly no fraternization between Czechs and Russians at this point.

Outside the village, children were busy picking baskets of purple plums from the loaded trees. The plums ripened all over Czechoslovakia just about the time of the invasion; whatever else happens, 1968 is going to be a bumper year for slivovitz, the national drink. There is only one public building in the village, a combined bar, restaurant, cinema and House of Culture. Here I found a good cross-section of the inhabitants, willing and even eager to talk to a Western journalist and tell me and my Czech interpreter how things had been going.

The people had been woken up about 4 a.m. on August 21 by the thunder of Russian tanks moving up the main road to Prague, a few hundred yards away. The tanks were going fast, with only their tiny blue convoy lights lit.

At first light they heard the ear-splitting whine of the heavy Russian transport aircraft overhead, on the final approach to Prague Airport. The people could easily make out the single red star on their tail fins. The size of this air armada was disturbing, but it could still, just possibly, be an unannounced manoeuvre.

But at 8 a.m. the first of the clandestine Czech radios came on the air, and the people heard, in the voices of Czech announcers whom they knew and trusted, the truth. About the same time the Russians' 'Radio Vltava'—actually the civil radio at Karl-Marx-Stadt in East Germany, just over the border—opened up with its version of events.

'Apart from the nonsense they were talking, they spoke bad Czech with heavy Russian accents,' said Vaclav, a burly miner. 'They were talking about the danger of counter-revolutionaries. We have no counter-revolutionaries here—everyone in the village is solidly behind our President and Mr Dubcek, and especially now. We have no Stalin people here, either' (by which he meant conservatives) 'or if there are any, they are hiding their faces.'

'We cannot tell you how good our radio and television have been,' said Ruzena, a farmer's wife built like a lady wrestler. There was general agreement to this in the bar. There were many references to Dubcek's moving phrase about 'the human face of socialism', and one man suggested that Dubcek should be proposed by the Czechs for the Nobel Peace Prize.

The village had a Czech national flag at half-mast outside each house. The villagers told me that these flags had been put out early on the Wednesday morning, when reliable news about the invasion had come through. 'We did not hold a meeting on the subject, and there were no orders,' said Vaclav. 'It just seemed the natural thing to do.'

The village had unusually few slogans and posters: only a few words on a neat sign on the local war memorial, 'Suverentia'—'Sovereignty'—and underneath, 'Dubcek, Svoboda, Vernost'—the last word is very emotive in Czech and means, roughly, 'faithful'. The effect of this simplicity was even more striking than the wild display of poster art, impassioned, witty, and sometimes downright vulgar, which I had just seen in Prague.

Life in the village had not been directly affected by the occupation as much as in the big cities, but the atmosphere of foreboding and anxiety was exactly the same. For the first week, the twenty or so villagers who work in Prague stayed home because of the chaos in the public transport system. But buses came every day, including the day of the invasion, to fetch the people who work in the steel mill and coalmine near Kladno. The post office in the village was closed from the first day of the invasion. This prevented people withdrawing their savings, and apart from food, no one in the village bought anything at all for several weeks, preferring to keep such cash as they had for emergencies. There was a run on tinned provisions at the general store for the first few days.

But, because there were no customers, the other shops were all shut, except for the barber's shop, open most nights to 9 or 10 p.m., and the bar at the House of Culture, where there were endless discussions. 'We are just not singing the same tune as the Russians,' said one farmer gloomily, 'and they have the big orchestra.'

It would be wrong to think that there was distress of a material kind in the village during the occupation. No one from the village had been harmed and no damage had been caused. In fact, no Russian had actually set foot inside the village limits; the only visitors in the early days of the occupation were an occasional carload of Czech soldiers driving through to see that all was well. The atmosphere was rather of anger, and fear for the future; the clock was likely to go back, the villagers agreed, but how far? And in this respect, the village I visited was very much the same as any other village in Czechoslovakia.

It was, in fact, different from other small places in only one important respect—it was almost certainly the only village in the whole country which did not change or obliterate its name. The name was still there, defiant and undefaced, when I arrived. 'We talked it over and decided that it would be wrong to conceal it,' said Vaclav. 'We thought that even the Russians would respect it. We suffered under Fascism with them, together. Why should they believe that Lidice has changed now?'

On June 10, 1942, in reprisal for the assassination in Prague of the Nazi 'Protector' of Bohemia and Moravia, Reinhard Heydrich, the Germans shot the entire male population of Lidice, deported the women and children to Ravensbruck concentration camp and levelled the village to the ground. The

people who live in the rebuilt Lidice are relatives of the victims
and a few children, now grown up, who survived the camps.
Among them are Ruzena and Vaclav.

7 THE RECKONING

On the night of Monday, August 26, there was an
atmosphere of gloom in Prague. The people stubbornly
continued their 'passive resistance'; after dark a group
of students defied the curfew and crept through the
silent streets putting up new signs forbidding the Russian
tanks to enter the main streets of the city. As they lay
in their beds, the people could hear the tanks crunching
about, moving away from their positions around Wenceslas Square and the news agency buildings. There
was apprehension in the air. The Czech leaders had not
returned, as promised, from Moscow. Were they being
put under further pressure? Had they been double-
crossed? Had they sold out? Where was Dubcek?

But at 4 a.m., by overnight plane, Svoboda,
Smrkovsky, Kriegel and Dubcek returned to Prague.
They looked pale and haggard, and were driven straight
to the Central Committee building. On the plane they
had discussed the only two choices left open to them: to
resign, or to face the people with the details of the Moscow agreement and try to secure popular support to
carry on as best they could under the terms of the
Kremlin's rulings. There are many who argue that
had they resigned, the Soviet Union would have been
totally unable to find quislings to form a puppet
regime, and would then have been forced to make a
more generous deal with Dubcek.

A leading figure in Czechoslovakia who saw Dubcek
after his return from Moscow told me:

'In many ways Dubcek is naïve, and too trusting. He

said: "We have made an agreement, and both the Russians and ourselves will keep it." I told him I thought this was foolish, that the Russians had no intention of keeping any agreement, and that he should leave, thus retaining the support of the people. Had he resigned the country would have ground to a halt with repercussions perhaps inside the Kremlin itself. The Russians would have been forced then to accept the kind of society that Czechoslovakia wants.'

Nobody knows just how strong the pressures were on Dubcek and his colleagues to quit, but by breakfast time they had decided to stay in office. Senior executives of the leading newspapers, radio and television stations and the official news agency, were given an off-the-record briefing by Mr Cernik, who outlined the agreement and how the new censorship rules would affect them. It was also reported in some newspapers, including the *New York Times*, *The Times* and the *Guardian*, that he advised the intellectuals and writers who had been prominent in the liberal reform movement to 'get out of the country while the going is good'. Later Cernik denied making such a statement, but it certainly led to a rush from the country.

At 10.30 a.m. Mr Smrkovsky arrived at the National Assembly; the deputies sang the National Anthem before his emotional speech confirming that the agreement had been a necessary compromise. There were shouts of protest and demands that he should tell the full story. Meanwhile the text of the agreement was made known; it included these points:

A phased withdrawal of Russian and other Warsaw Pact countries' forces 'would take place as the situation in Czechoslovakia normalizes itself', subject to the stationing of two Soviet divisions on the West German border.

The Czechoslovak leadership would continue in office despite Moscow's earlier, bitter condemnation.

The reform programme agreed in January 1968 would continue, but controls would be instituted over information and press comment, particularly comment on Warsaw Pact countries.

A loan of an unspecified amount and duration would be provided by the Soviet Union to pay for the damage caused by the invasion.

The ambiguous wording of the agreement at once aroused anxiety and bitter disappointment. The Russians had refused to recognize the secret extraordinary Congress of the Czechoslovak Communist Party held in the electronics factory outside Prague during the first days of the invasion, and instead of accepting the liberal Central Committee elected then, was only prepared to consider the meeting as a 'consultation' of Congress delegates.

This was important, for it meant that the re-election of Dubcek as First Secretary of the Party had been revoked, and it put his political future into the hands of the *next* Congress, that is the Congress *after* the Moscow agreement. Even more worrying, however, was the use of the word 'normalize' in the agreement over the withdrawal of the bulk of the Warsaw Pact troops. It became clear the troops would remain in the country just as long as the Kremlin wished. During mid-morning the tension mounted as people gathered in groups round transistor radios for the agonizing wait until in late afternoon President Svoboda's voice came on the air. He spoke slowly, formally, as he said that senseless bloodshed had to be avoided at all costs, and that the only realistic future was moral and intellectual resistance. In his solemn words the tragic impotence of the Czechoslovaks in the face of the situation could be clearly felt; fear was not the only motive for the decision. People wept as he said:

'As a soldier I know what bloodshed can be caused in a conflict between civilians and an army with modern equipment. Consequently, as your President, I considered it my duty to do all I could to ensure that this does not happen, that the blood of peoples who have always been friends is not spilled senselessly, and that at the same time the fundamental interests of our fatherland and its people are safeguarded. I do not want to hide the fact that painful sores caused by these events will long remain.'

After Svoboda's speech the mood in Prague changed. Defiance, albeit gloomy and touched with foreboding, gave way to disillusionment. The older people felt that such a compromise was inevitable in such a desperate situation, and perhaps remembered the hopelessness of Hungary. But the younger people reacted with rage. They tore about the city in fast-moving cars, scattering leaflets into the streets from open windows.

Nearly three hours later, Dubcek spoke to the nation. His broadcast was announced by the opening bars of Beethoven's Fifth Symphony, with their 'V for Victory' call. His voice shook with suppressed emotion and exhaustion. It was hard to believe that this was a Communist leader speaking, for here was a man actually appealing to the people, a phenomenon almost unheard of behind the Iron Curtain. This was no four hour dissertation by a drab figure in a drab suit reading a carefully prepared script; this was the voice of passion from a human being, a terrible cry for help from a man who had come to love being in the popular eye. Yet there was heart-rending sincerity too—the broadcast was interrupted frequently as Dubcek broke down and his voice gave way to tears.

He pleaded that the only possible way to save the nation from disaster was to maintain strict discipline and order, and to keep faith. Withdrawal of the Russian troops depended almost entirely on the maintenance of public order and on the absence of open provocation; to bring about the speediest 'normalization', censorship would have to be temporarily imposed. Then he passionately emphasized that at all costs the unity of the people and the Party had to be safeguarded:

'I believe, and I say this to your face, that in our life we cannot and will not act otherwise than to work according to the ideals of our people. In this difficult situation there is nothing left to us but to exert all our strength, our reason, so as to be truly able to carry out our future work. A nation in which everyone will be guided by reason and conscience will not perish.'

Dubcek's broadcast was repeated many times on the free radio. The first broadcast was live and revealed the true circumstances in which it took place. A Czechoslovak who heard it writes: 'Several times Dubcek seemed almost to faint in front of the microphone. His speech was heavy, with long extended pauses. You could hear his breathing, the breathing of a sick, beaten man. It gave the impression that he was not only at the end of his strength, but even that he was being subjected to physical force during the actual broadcast, that there was someone urging him to get on with the text. Dubcek gave little hints to try and make people understand the position. Several times he used Czech or Russian words, even though he was speaking, as he always does, in Slovak. At certain moments he seemed to get back his will to act. After long stretches of mechanical reading, he would begin using his old style. But such moments were always followed by long pauses. In the broadcasts that followed, of course, all these pauses were removed from the tape.'

People glimpsed Dubcek looking pale and beaten, a bandage round one arm and another round his head. When he spoke it was not from the normal studios, which were occupied and cut off from the transmitters, but from Hradcany Palace. The Russians had set up the broadcast and had had to ask for it to go out on the underground 'Free' radio, whose transmitters they had not yet managed to locate. For Dubcek to speak on their own Radio Vltava would have given quite the wrong impression. Even so, there is strong evidence that Dubcek was still under physical arrest at this time. His mother revealed in a radio interview days later that her son had still not been able to communicate with her from Prague, that there was no explanation for this other than that his movements were controlled.

Despite Dubcek's efforts, the people were not convinced. Thousands gathered in Wenceslas Square, and marched, twenty-five abreast, on the Parliament buildings, shouting: 'We don't want to live on our knees. We want the whole truth.' Cars and lorries sounded their horns in a 15-minute burst of pent-up feeling. Demonstrators ripped up portraits of Dubcek and Svoboda.

A deputy appeared at a first floor window and said: 'Parliament will not endorse any agreement that is against our freedom to speak and to write, or against our sovereignty.' There was a roar of approval as he added: 'Parliament does not agree with the Moscow communique. We will do our best to make this republic democratic, sovereign and free.'

Russian tanks slid, like boa constrictors, back into the main streets. There was some shooting. In the square in front of the National Assembly, the Russians seemed about to fire when an anxious deputy ran out of the building and calmed the demonstrators by assuring them that the Assembly would not accept a settlement which would allow the Soviet forces to remain indefinitely in Prague. The radio stations broadcast urgent appeals for responsible conduct; slowly the crowds began to disperse and the tanks rumbled off.

Withdrawal of Soviet tanks from the streets of the principal cities lent at least a semblance of normality to the country, but the Russian presence was felt by every citizen. In the Ministry of Culture harassed government

79

officials struggled to prepare new press laws, and to provide for the reimposition of censorship. The police—and the secret police—were working out how to make the other special measures agreed in Moscow effective: the curbs on freedom of association and freedom of speech, the travel restrictions, and the regulation that public meetings 'contrary to foreign political interests and public order' could be dispersed by the police.

The sad Czechs were assured that there would be no return to the harsh oppression of Stalinist days, and that punishment would be meted out by civilian judges in accordance with Czechoslovak law—no mean promise in the face of the threat posed by the 1,500 Czech-speaking Soviet K.G.B. agents said to be roaming the country. According to the underground newspapers, the K.G.B. men were arriving daily by train from Moscow. One newspaper, *Svobodny Legalni*, listed the registration numbers of the cars that the K.G.B. were said to be using—some Russian Volgas, a few British Ford Cortinas. Yet, if the K.G.B. were active, there was no concrete evidence of it, and no arrests. Intellectuals, including the outspoken Mr Kamil Winter, head of Czech Television News, continued to leave the country. He and his wife drove to Austria with their car piled high with holiday gear and were stopped only twice by Russian soldiers, who did not ask any questions or search the car. In retrospect it seems likely that the Soviet Union were pleased to see the intellectuals leaving the country; it provided them with good propaganda material claiming that the 'counter-revolutionaries' had fled.

Even if the Czechs were treated reasonably well during these later days of occupation, they regarded the presence of Soviet soldiers as a bitter pill. But the leaders warned they would have to swallow the pill if they wanted to salvage parts of the original Action Programme and a measure of national independence.

To put these so-called 'temporary unpopular' measures in perspective, the country's liberal leaders made an unprecedented proclamation guaranteeing the freedom of law-abiding citizens and promising that the liberalization programme should not be scrapped.

The signatories—Party leader Mr Dubcek, President Svoboda, Prime Minister Cernik, Mr Smrkovsky, the Speaker, and Mr Husak, the Slovak Party's First Secretary—also appealed to the intellectuals who had fled the country to come home. 'Your place is here, we are waiting for you. The Republic needs you and your skills', the proclamation said, revealing the concern of the liberal leadership over the exodus of intellectuals engineered by the Soviet secret police through direct threats and false rumours of impending mass arrests.

And so the struggle to fend off total military occupation without betraying the nation continued. On August 29 there was a conference of Czechoslovak Communist Party and Government leaders to try and find a compromise leadership that would be acceptable both to the people and to Moscow. It was not an easy task, but in the end a new Praesidium was proposed which included Dubcek, Cernik, Smrkovsky, Simon and Spacek—the five who made the traumatic trip to Moscow—and some of those whom the Kremlin had hoped would form a puppet government: Barbirek, Rigo, and Sadovsky. Kriegel, whom the Russians particularly hated, was quietly dropped. There were more speeches, 'I tell you frankly that—despite all the help we have had from our friends—of whom we now have many, and whom I thank from the bottom of my heart—our country, in the situation that now obtains in the world, has no real guarantee and no hope other than its own good sense and, above all, its unity.'

It was this unity that the Russians were obviously trying to crack, by seeking the co-operation of Mr

Gustav Husak, the Slovakian Party First Secretary, and by unsuccessful appeals to Slovak nationalism. There had been reports that the Soviet leaders had given the Czechoslovaks the choice of acceptance of their terms or facing the declaration of an independent Slovak state and the establishment of a military government in Bohemia and Moravia.

Hour by hour the Russians mounted more pressure on Dubcek as he struggled to get the country going again. They ordered Prime Minister Cernik to make rooms available in government offices for Russian 'advisors'. The prospect of more advisors was a grim one, and took the Czechoslovaks back to the very worst years of the 1950s. They had first got rid of Russian advisors during the de-Stalinization period under Kruschev, and the few that had remained in the Ministries of Defence and Interior were sent back in January 1968 when the role of Soviet agents in previous trials and purges had become widely known.

The secret radio stations were given orders to cease attacking the occupying forces, but *Literani Listy* put out a manifesto called: 'No compromise with censorship', and also published a cartoon showing a Russian soldier in a tank saying: 'Workers of the world unite—or I'll shoot.'

Some Czechs optimistically took the mention of a Russian withdrawal at an unspecified future time to mean that they had won, but groups of students, assessing more realistically the meaning of the phrase 'a return to normal life', toured the city tossing from speeding cars a duplicated sheet with the single word 'TREASON'. And someone painted up outside the apartment of one of the conservatives still absent in Moscow: 'The traitor Indra lives here on the 5th floor.'

Life was certainly returning to some sort of uneasy normality by the second weekend of the invasion. The daily hour-long general strikes came to an end, banks and shops re-opened, people went back to work—and the Russians began digging themselves in in the Prague parks.

A belated Russian propaganda campaign got under way. They finally launched an occupation newspaper, *Zpravy* ('News'), printed in East Germany and dropped from helicopter over the city. The Czechs simply stuffed them into wastepaper baskets and set them on fire; and after two days of feeding smoking rubbish bins *Zpravy* ceased publication.

The posters and slogans came down from the walls of Prague, and the Russians were quick to eliminate the last vestiges of public protest. For many days Czechs kept a non-stop vigil with lowered national and black flags before the statue of the Good Wenceslas. A banner carried a prayer 'for the souls of the Czechoslovak dead' to the saint. On Tuesday, September 3, the Russians told the Prague police that unless the demonstrations were stopped and further demonstrations made impossible, they would come with tanks and do the job themselves. The vigil group took down their flags and their banner, and a working party completely covered the base of the statue with shrubs in tubs, dumped a ton of earth on the road round the statue, and planted zinnias. This impromptu, striking addition to the beauties of the city is now watered every day by a Czech fire engine.

On Thursday, September 5, Colonel-General Pavlovsky ordered an ambitious programme aimed at the hearts and minds of the Czechoslovak people. Like most such military endeavours, it was not very successful. A Soviet colonel called at the C.Z.M. motorcycle factory in Strakonice and got an icy rebuff to his offer to send an officer to explain Soviet policy to the workers. Another colonel who called at a factory near Prague with a bottle of vodka was told by the manager that Czechs never drank spirits during office hours. The Russian then offered the service of his men for any odd jobs that might be going; making tea, sweeping out the factory, oiling machinery or tidying up the grounds. He got a frosty refusal. In other parts of the country, Soviet officers tried to press their troops on to the Czechs to help them with the harvest, but were politely told that the Czechs had been managing for centuries without Russian assistance.

The Russians vacated the television studios on Tuesday, September 3, and the next night Czech television came cautiously back on the air from its own studios. The first face to appear was the classically beautiful one of Kamila Mouskova, who has been reading the news since Czech television began twelve years ago. Mrs Mouskova played a prominent part in the clandestine television broadcasts. Some glimpse of what 'normalization' was going to mean was shown by the early programmes made in the invisible cage of a censorship which had not yet been imposed. Most of the evening was taken up with a long documentary about children going back to school and a filmed version of the Smetana opera *Dalibor*. Even the latter was a second thought: the programme planners had originally scheduled the Czech composer's opera *My Country*, but at the last minute they feared that this might not be 'normal' enough for the Russians.

Official censors were appointed to radio and television. On Sunday night, September 8, the new censor of television, Josef Vohnout, took the unusual step of appearing on television himself to talk about his new job, in a new programme called 'We are with you, you are with us'—which happened to be the call sign of the clandestine television service. The programme also featured the pop singer Karol Cernoch, singing a new number called 'I hope this is just a bad dream', and the poet Jaroslav Seifert, who recited a poem in which he suggested that the last Soviet tank to leave Czechoslovakia should be set up as a monument, alongside the first Soviet tank to arrive in the city in 1945.

This programme, seemingly a fairly normal variety offering, pleased Mr Vohnout. Prime Minister Cernik also told the television people that he liked the show. But the Soviet Ambassador, Mr S. V. Cervonenko, did not like it at all. He telephoned Cernik and complained. The next night 'We are with you, you are with us' was replaced by a film about hiking in Central Slovakia. It has not been on the air since and a sign went up in a main office of the television building: 'Experimental Psychiatric Clinic'.

Meanwhile the Kremlin was showing signs of increasing displeasure and exasperation with Dubcek, and for talks on the economy invited to Moscow Mr Cernik, the Prime Minister, instead of the First Secretary, as is the usual custom. Cernik met Mr Breshnev, Mr Kosygin and Mr Podgorny, and signed a number of economic agreements clearly intended to increase Russia's financial stranglehold on Czechoslovakia.

Czechoslovakia was already purchasing from the Soviet Union 99.5 per cent of her oil, 90.3 per cent of her wheat, 83.6 per cent of her iron ore, 53.3 per cent of other metals, and 53.6 per cent of her cotton. Two-thirds of her foreign trade was already with Comecon countries—but this was clearly not enough for Moscow. The leaders in the Kremlin told Cernik that Prague would have to raise her trade with Comecon to a total of 80 per cent, thus slashing trade with the West.

The effect of this on Czechoslovakia's future can only be the subject of guesswork. To say the least, the rejection of badly needed Western credits and know-how will increase the country's already formidable economic difficulties. The hopes for Mr Dubcek's Action Programme, which remain inseparable from a thriving national economy, are slim indeed. But perhaps more important than anything, Cernik's agreement with the Kremlin frustrates the bold economic reforms planned by the man whose ideas had been at the very root of the fundamental new thinking which germinated in Czechoslovakia during those exciting months prior to the invasion.

That man is Dr Ota Sik.

8 THE REFORMER

Tanks; flags red with the blood of patriots; tragic tales of savagery, misunderstanding, power struggles and exile; the deep-driving question among Communists on whether a member of the socialist brotherhood has the right to self-determination, and among the countries of the outside world on what the Czech crisis will mean to the future of Communism. August 21, 1968, has disgorged them all. But deep in the heart of the events leading up to that fateful day, and since, lies a profound problem: the fact of a country once industrially advanced and economically resilient, but within that socialist brotherhood, barely escaping economic ruin.

Communism remains basically an economic philosophy. By the mid 1950s, when the Stalinist-tailored war economics, with their stress on heavy industry to the exclusion of consumer goods, began to cause widespread discontent, it was clear that there must be drastic economic change. Yugoslavia was the first to move, after breaking with the Kremlin in 1948, and introduced a system of decentralized planning and 'workers' councils' to co-manage its factories. In 1956 the Polish 'bread and freedom' riots in Poznan triggered reforms which—on paper, at least—even outstripped those in Yugoslavia. Soon, in Moscow, Evsei Liberman was talking of 'incentives' and 'profit motives'. This set the Eastern bloc—Hungary, Bulgaria, and even the Stalinist states of Czechoslovakia and East Germany—

thinking of reforms, of bonuses and reinvestment, of free prices, incentives, and even that capitalist notion, the accumulation of wealth.

No East European economy suffered so painfully under Stalinism as Czechoslovakia. It was the 'machine shop' of the Eastern bloc; forced by Moscow to make machine tools and weapons that the Soviets needed but for which they gave insignificant reinvestment. Czechoslovak economic growth, booming at 8 per cent in 1949, had slumped so far by 1963 that it was actually in decline—a state unheard of in a planned economy.

No one has been more acutely conscious of the economic disaster than another long-time Party member, who from 1941 to 1945 survived the Nazi concentration camp at Mauthausen, where Novotny was also imprisoned. He is Professor Ota Sik (pronounced Sheek), former Director of the Institute of Economics at the Czechoslovak Academy of Sciences, and mastermind of the Czechoslovakian economic reforms, who was second only to Dubcek in the recent Czech popularity polls.

It was Novotny, then acting as President of Czechoslovakia and First Secretary, who originally approved Professor Sik's plans for thorough surgery on the Czech economy in 1965. But as the months went by, Professor Sik became convinced that application of the reforms would never be more than half-hearted as long as Stalinists held the country. He believed efficient economic reform could be achieved only with political reform. So with Dubcek, Smrkovsky and the progressives, he worked for the ousting of Novotny.

Ota Sik, barely more than 5ft 4in in height, has a wide, dimpled smile, solid, wide shoulders, and an even wider reputation as a first-class economist. He was born on September 11, 1919, in the Bohemian town of Teplice, the former Teplitz, hard on the East

German border, not far from Dresden, an area where German and Czech have intermingled and both languages are widely used. Sik himself is the son of a German-Jew and a Czech mother. His father was a factory worker.

At five Ota was sent to the local school, and a friend who followed him one year behind through primary, grammar and college (secondary) education says he was 'a nice boy, well-behaved and popular'.

He began to study political ecomony while still at college, but he learned most of his economics as a Party man after the war. Like Dubcek, he worked for the resistance movement against the Nazis, but was caught and imprisoned for four years. He was elected to the Central Committee of the C.C.P. as candidate in 1958 and full member in 1962. But by the beginning of the 1960s the burning interest of this grey-eyed, vigorous dumpling—described by Czech and foreign acquaintances alike as a modest and sincere man—had become, not a career in politics, but economics.

Before becoming Director of the Academy's Institute of Economics in 1962, he lectured on political economy at many universities and colleges. He is chairman of the Czechoslovak Economic Society and in 1965 was elected to the Committee of the International Economic Association, which has its headquarters in Paris.

As long ago as 1957 he had become seriously concerned at the 'economic antagonisms' generated by Soviet policies: the gross imbalance which could occur between supply and demand; the languid demeanour they produced in the labour force. His criticisms were shrugged off by the Stalinists. But he pressed on, with a 20-man investigating committee, discussing the problems with political and trade union officials, with rank and file Communists, and with non-Party people.

Professor Sik drew the conclusions that 'The overwhelming majority felt that the old system of management, based mainly on directives from central bodies handed down the administrative ladder, had to be replaced.'

On paper he was able to demonstrate that Czechoslovakia's economy had progressed since liberation from Nazi occupation and the imposition of Communist rule—in 1963 the national income had increased to 160 per cent of the 1937 level; industrial output had increased nearly five-fold. But pre-war Czechoslovakia already ranked high among the world's industrially developed countries.

'Now,' warned Professor Sik, 'the emphasis on extensive rather than intensive development has resulted in a lag in efficiency. Rigid centralized planning and management have become the main impediments to greater efficiency.'

In December 1963 his committee demanded a thorough shake-up of the country's economy. The reforms they proposed were startling, especially in the most firmly Stalinist satellite. But in 1965 Novotny himself and the Central Committee approved the changes.

Novotny, a rigid extremist, had always opposed Sik's ideas; but faced with virtual economic collapse and no alternative solution, he and the Central Committee were forced reluctantly to agree to Sik's proposals. It was quite a victory for the progressives: the *apparatchiks*, with their limited Communist qualifications, naturally wanted to retain their power and privileges, and were afraid of the younger, more capable economists like Sik.

Since 1948 more than 250,000 Soviet-type Party functionaries had been created and placed in commanding posts on the strength of their political loyalty alone; they fought tooth and nail against the reforms which would endanger the positions and prestige for which many of them were not equipped.

To be effective the new economic structure needed a profound change in the thinking of all who held positions of responsibility, not only at the top, but right through every level of administration.

This was a major aim of Ludvik Vaculik's 2,000-word Writers' Manifesto of June 27. The manifesto was not, as it has often been interpreted, an anti-Communist document, but a plea for democratic socialist participation in the running of the country by the whole population, especially for those living in areas beyond Prague, instead of mere passive submission to orders from a Government sealed off in splendid isolation from the people. The effectiveness of the manifesto was demonstrated in the following weeks when the people united in protest against the threat of foreign infiltration into their national affairs. The man in the street felt as involved in the crisis as those at the top: this was shown in the two million signatures collected in the streets in support of the Czech leaders against the Russian claims during the conference in Cierna; in the Republican Fund to which the country's wives and widows gave their ear-rings, rings, brooches and bracelets to improve the nation's gold reserves.

Having gained official sanction, Ota Sik, the outspoken Pilsener, proceeded to say exactly what was rotten in the state of Czechoslovakia. State investments, he said, were expended on building *new* factories and producing and installing *additional* machines. This left less and less for renewal and modernization of existing plants, which, as they grew older and more infirm, gave diminishing returns. Secondly, technological advances were ignored with such ostrich-like stupidity that the growth of labour productivity had practically ceased in 1962–3.

Instead of improving efficiency, the country had augmented the labour force, by recruiting among housewives and agricultural employees. 'But when these auxiliary sources were exhausted,' said Professor Sik, 'it became more imperative than ever to place the emphasis on higher productivity.' He criticized the enlistment of housewives as industrial workers before adequate provision of public services, such as creches, nursery schools, school canteens, and so on. Above all, he said, the rapid transfer of part of the agricultural labour force to industry had taken place before mechanization and the use of chemicals had been adopted sufficiently to compensate for the outflow of manpower. Nor had enough attention been paid to foreign trade. Although the country had a relatively advanced industry, it had to import much of its raw material. The home market was too slight to encourage the growth of efficient mass production which, however, was necessary if Czechoslovakia's goods were to compete abroad. The position was aggravated by the fact that Czechoslovakia was not self-supporting in agricultural products. A healthier trade balance, according to Professor Sik, was vital to economic progress. Even worse, the output of less essential and sometimes unnecessary items was expanding, while the list of goods in short supply grew longer and longer.

Centralized planning, he alleged, was setting the enterprises quantitative targets at the neglect of quality; was using funds and materials uneconomically; was encouraging plants to produce goods regardless of whether or not they were actually needed; and was strangling some factories because there was no way of ensuring they were supplied with necessary components.

A year later, at the Thirteenth Congress of the Czechoslovak Communist Party in June 1966, it was decided to introduce the new economic policy. Though none of it represented a return to capitalism, Novotny and the Old Guard did not like any of it, because they knew that it would mean that the 'workers'—who previously had received the same pay no matter how diligently or how indolently they laboured—would have to work harder. And these workers, schooled by the Party bureaucracy to believe that Party policies were primarily concerned with their interests, were a main source of power for Novotny and the Old Guard. On the other hand, there would be a better deal for farmers and 'intellectuals'. No longer would a hard working doctor or teacher with years of hard-gained qualifications and experience, receive no more than the laziest factory worker.

The new management system shattered the rigidity and anachronisms of central planning. It eliminated subsidies and forced each Czechoslovak factory to pay its way or close down. Incentives were to be introduced. Instead of simply transferring all gross income (profits) to the State, as under Soviet-type Communism, only a part of the gross income was to be transferred in the form of taxes. The remainder would belong to the enterprise involved, Skoda plant, brewery and glass factory alike; the Party economists in Prague were to assume a function similar to Western investment analysts, and it was to be left to the individual managers to decide for themselves how much to reinvest for future development and how much to pay out to employees as bonuses. Thus, there would be a profit incentive.

If the workers created a highly successful enterprise, they might receive up to 20 per cent of their total wages as bonuses. On the other hand, Professor Sik's plan guaranteed only 92 per cent of the State-set wage, so that if a plant became inefficient or the workers indolent, they would suffer pay setbacks.

Said Sik: 'If the system is to work it needs real market prices. Only a few staples [mainly foodstuffs and fuel] will have fixed prices. All others will be allowed to move freely in response to supply and demand.'

The new economy also planned to force specialization in Czechoslovak industry. 'At present we produce

78 per cent of the world spectrum of types of machinery. This is impossible for such a small country,' explained Professor Sik. By November 1966 some 1300 redundant factories had been closed and another 1400 were possibly to shut down.

The impact on managers was strong. Instead of handing out fat subsidies, the Czech Central Bank was told to charge a 6 per cent interest on capital loans— a move calculated to make plant managers eager to develop in the right direction. The Czechs immediately established Western-style business management schools to teach the new economic skills to managers who previously had been unaware even of world market prices of the goods they were supposed to produce.

Throughout 1967 the economic reform showed few results, for it was being mangled in the leadership struggle between radicals and conservatives. Towards the end of the year Ota Sik told a Yugoslav journalist that the compromise 'extorted from us' would have to be annulled. On December 19, at a grim, angry session of the full Central Committee of the Czechoslovak Communist Party, Professor Ota Sik rose to speak first. He denounced the Old Guard, demanded that Central Committee members should be allowed to form themselves into distinct sections (thus creating in-party opposition), and called for political liberalization as well as economic reform.

As soon as Sik sat down, Novotnyites sprang up to make bitter personal attacks upon him, but Josef Smrkovsky, the old resistance leader who had suffered personally under Novotny but who remains one of the most trusted men in Czechoslovak politics, made a speech which won over many of the waverers. On December 22 the meeting was adjourned until January 5, the day that Novotny of the Old Guard lost the struggle for power.

The Central Committee decreed that development of heavy industry, the fetish of Communist conservatives, should be slowed down and the capital saved diverted to implement the long battled-for economic reforms; that working hours would be reduced gradually from 44 a week to $42\frac{1}{2}$; that wages were to grow at 3·8 per cent annually, while the cost of living was not to rise at more than 1·5 per cent a year.

Novotny and Sik had been close friends during their survival together in Mauthausen, but as the burly Sik developed into an academic with a world-wide reputation, and the willowy Novotny into a hard-line Party functionary, their differing views drove them so far apart that they became arch-opponents. Nevertheless, Sik could have gone into the Government while Novotny was still in power, but it was not until January 1968, when Dubcek became First Secretary and Oldrich Cernik Prime Minister, that he agreed to accept a government post. Cernik, an engineer and former conservative, had come to support Sik's plans for economic reform. So Ota Sik resigned as Director of the Institute of Economics and became one of the Government's three Deputy Premiers.

In June 1968, ready with thick black-rimmed glasses and a sheaf of notes to which he almost never referred, Ota Sik, as Deputy Premier of Czechoslovakia and member of the Economic Planning Commission, faced the television cameras and the nation. In a series of six lectures, he twice a week presented the people with a sober analysis of the Czech economy, speaking utterly without the affectations of politician or orator, and with an air almost of pessimism.

The outlook, he said, was not encouraging: in the next seven years Czechoslovakia could not hope to do more than recover a ruined economy. There would be only a little progress in social services and housing. As to foreign aid, an initial investment of 500 million dollars would be needed merely to eliminate the consequences of the Stalinist policies. (Before World War II, 90 per cent of Czechoslovakia's exports went to Western countries; now 70 per cent go to socialist countries, mainly the U.S.S.R. German experts estimate that Russia owes 800 million dollars to Czechoslovakia, mainly for machinery and weapons.)

Dr Sik performed a miracle. With simple logic, he presented his case so that it was understood at all levels of society, and appreciated by agricultural workers as well as the country's leading economists. But the next chapter was less encouraging.

At the time of the invasion Deputy Premier Sik was in Belgrade. So too were Foreign Minister Jiri Hajek, Frantisek Vlasak, the Minister of Economic Planning, Professor J. Trokan, Minister of Public Works, and Stefan Gasparik, President of the Czechoslovak State Control Commission. Two days later Sik, Vlasak and Gasparik were in Bucharest for talks with Rumanian President Nicolae Ceausescu. Before their departure from Belgrade they had signed an appeal urging the world's Communist parties to help the Czechoslovak Party and people.

The next day, August 24, *Pravda* published a blacklist: Ota Sik was named for his 'heretical views on socialist economics'. Soon after the Moscow agreement, Professor Sik resigned from his post as Deputy Premier, and it was reported that he had been appointed as an economic counsellor to the Czechoslovak Embassy in Yugoslavia. However, the embassy quickly denied that such a permanent appointment had been made. Nor would they confirm Dr Sik's whereabouts. In the second week in September he was reported to have arrived for a brief stay in Zurich and a self-exiled Czech, who until the invasion held a high post in Czechoslovakia, claimed to have met Sik in Vienna a few days later, on September 14.

The *Tass* announcement of Sik's resignation from the post of Deputy Premier, published in *Pravda* and *Izvestia* on September 5, denounced him as 'a right-wing revisionist closely allied to the counter-revolution', and accused him of meeting in Belgrade with Jiri Hajek—Novotny's Minister of Education and, until September 19, Foreign Minister under Dubcek—to prepare 'a temporary committee ready to take over the functions of an exile government'.

The Soviet accusations against Dr Sik produced a bold move by thirteen of Czechoslovakia's most eminent economists, many of them of international reputation, who took the considerable risk of writing a letter in defence of Sik published in Prague's *Rude Pravo* on September 16:

'In the "Letters of Five Communist Workers' Parties to the Central Committee of the Czechoslovak Communist Party" [the Warsaw letter written by the U.S.S.R., East Germany, Poland, Bulgaria and Hungary] it is stated: "We do not interfere in the methods of economic planning and management of socialist economy of Czechoslovakia or in your decisions aiming at the perfection of the economic structure in the development of socialist democracy." We wish to state that we are convinced that if this declaration were respected it could help towards the amelioration of relationships among the socialist countries.'

But the outlook for Professor Sik is serious, since he has the added disadvantage of being Jewish. It would not be at all surprising if the Russians were to blame the Czechoslovak liberalization drive on 'Zionism'. Indeed, Czech exiles suggest that Dubcek himself asked Professor Sik to resign for fear of anti-Zionist purges. Within weeks of the invasion there were already pointers that perhaps, yet again, Jews might be made the scapegoats. There was the appalling treatment of Mr Kriegel in

Moscow, and the fact that Dr Goldstuecker, leader of the Writers' Union, was in the *Pravda* blacklist. The Russians also promised to provide 'all the necessary evidence' for the trial of 'Zionist counter-revolutionaries'.

One does not have to look far for precedents. The Polish leadership blamed the liberal stirring in March 1968 on Zionism. Less than two decades ago there was a series of purges of people charged with Zionism in Hungary, Albania and Bulgaria, culminating in the most terrible of all in Czechoslovakia in 1952. Officially about twenty were executed, but unofficially it is estimated that up to 40,000 Jews disappeared, were deported or thrown into prison.

In the weeks leading to his resignation, Czechoslovakia's liberal-minded Foreign Minister under Dubcek, Dr Hajek, was subjected to vicious attacks in the Russian press, including the false accusation that he was a Jew who had changed his name, and who had assisted the Gestapo during the wartime occupation of Czechoslovakia. However, on the day that Dr Hajek's resignation was made known in Prague, it was announced that Russia had apologized for its allegations that Dr Hajek had been a Nazi agent. Mr Kuznetsov, the Soviet Deputy Foreign Minister, said that the allegation had been due to 'misinformation': Dr Hajek had been arrested by the Gestapo and sentenced to twelve years' imprisonment in 1940.

Ota Sik has devoted his life since 1945 to understanding the problems of socialist economics, and is the architect of a pattern to save his country from ruin while embodying the socialist principles in which he believes. When on July 15, 1968, he went with his wife Lilka to Lancaster University's Ashton Hall to receive an honorary degree of Doctor of Laws from Princess Alexandra, and to attend a two-hour seminar with staff of the Economics Department, he was described by the Vice-Chancellor as 'a very intelligent and practical economist, who has given a great deal of thought to the circumstances of his own country. He spoke (in a strong accent and with considerable bother with English idiom) with great enthusiasm, and nearly always about Czechoslovakia. He is a modest man; a very pleasant person indeed.'

Because the failure of the old hard-line Stalinism was more spectacular in Czechoslovakia than in any other Eastern bloc economy, success with Professor Ota Sik's sweeping reforms could well point a searchlight on the economies of all Communism. But failure could well bring the heavy jackboot of centralism crashing down again.

9 IVAN IN PRAGUE

The invasion of Czechoslovakia offered one unexpected bonus for correspondents; it was the first time Western observers had seen the Red Army in action since the invasion of Hungary in 1956. The Czechoslovak operation was conducted in a glare of publicity. Correspondents were able to take advantage of a rare opportunity to examine Soviet equipment and to talk reasonably freely with Soviet officers and private soldiers. Murray Sayle found it a first-class army, well equipped and well disciplined:

Ivan Ivanovitch comes from Tashkent or Odessa or perhaps Leningrad—in the latter case he is more than likely an officer. He is tall and blond; or sometimes unmistakably an Armenian, dark and jowly, like a young Nubar Gulbenkian; or often he has the dead black straight hair and narrow eyes of Mongolia; because this is a fully integrated army and like most armies it is

the farm boys and the country cousins who find themselves in the front line.

Half of the Soviet army of occupation came from
East Germany, and their tanks and trucks had East
German number-plates. The rest seemed to have come
straight from Russia, and their markings were in the
Cyrillic alphabet. But wherever he came from, Ivan
was lonely and bored in Prague, and his head was
spinning from endless ideological arguments. Despite
the lush display of consumer goods in Prague shops all
he wanted to do was to go home.

Ivan was roughly but serviceably equipped. The
infantry wore field boots (with woollen socks), whipcord
breeches (with underpants), whipcord combat jackets
(no undershirt) and forage caps. They wore a webbing
belt with an olive green buckle and an embossed star,
and an enamelled red star in their caps.

The infantrymen had steel helmets and were armed
with AK47 assault rifles. The Soviet army appears to
have dispensed altogether with conventional bolt-action
military rifles, except for a few snipers who carry high-
powered rifles in canvas covers. The NCOs had pistols
in wooden holsters and the officers carried automatic
pistols, similar to an American ·45.

The tank crews had black leather jackets and padded
helmets. The tanks, T34s and the enormous T54s, were
equipped with infra-red searchlights, which were not
on the tanks supplied by the Russians to Egypt for the
Middle East war in 1967. The tanks carried large
cylinders behind the turret, which many Western observers took to be spare fuel tanks, but in fact they
contain a roll of strong wooden matting to assist a
bogged-down tank to get out of mud.

A noticeable feature of the invasion was the mechanical reliability of the Russian equipment. The invasion
of Czechoslovakia was, from the military point of view,
a combined operation: three days after the first wave

arrived a division of Russian marines turned up, headed by a Soviet admiral magnificent in a white uniform and a technicolour array of medals. The marines wore their new uniform of khaki, with blue and white striped shirt and purple beret. There are few navigable waters in Czechoslovakia, and no beaches so the marines were given jobs guarding the Soviet monument.

The main Russian military base at Prague was the airport, which was turned into a fortified camp. Here Colonel-General Ivan Pavlovsky, the Soviet commander, was living in a mobile headquarters. The main Russian strongpoint within Prague itself was the Vrchlickeho Park, opposite the main railway station. This was completely taken over. A dozen T34 tanks and a squadron of armoured-cars were posted there, and amid this hardware Ivan and his comrades were living.

They began the day with reveille, in the form of a tug on the shoulder, at 5 a.m. The officers were sleeping in tents and the other ranks slept on the ground under waterproof capes. In the first few days of the occupation the Russians arrived with three days' combat rations, and when these were gone some went hungry for another two or three days. After a few days' confusion, the Russian commissariat began to function in an austere, but efficient fashion. At about 6 a.m. food arrived from the airport in field kitchens towed by lorries. Breakfast was *kasha*, millet porridge. Lunch was pea soup with lard floating on top. Dinner was bread – one loaf between four men per day, weighed up on elaborate and very Russian scales. Coffee twice a day and ten Russian cigarettes a day. There was no Russian Naafi, no PX and no parcels from home. One Russian trooper had not had a woman in three and a half years and no home leave for nearly four years. He had completed his three years' military service in East Germany, but because he was a 'specialist', he had been kept in the Army since January, 'since this whole thing began'.

Since Prague was in principle swarming with danger-ous counter-revolutionaries, the Russian soldiers got no leave and only appeared outside their Vrchlickeho Park camp in armed patrols or in armoured-cars. They spent their days washing their underclothes, cleaning weapons, and in endless political discussions with Czechs through the perimeter wire.

Their only recreation was a musical performance every afternoon in the children's playground. The Russian army of occupation arrived in Prague with three military bands, but their instruments remained in their boxes. The first performance of a more modest group of soldier dancers and musicians attracted an audience of two Czechs, both under four. Later shows were better attended—the Russian singing, dancing and accordion playing is, of course, marvellous—and as soon as a crowd of Czechs, looking for an argument, had assembled, the *Tass* cameraman climbed the chil-dren's slide for pictures of happy fraternization. An armed sentry stood at the entrance of the playground, keeping a watchful lookout for counter-revolutionaries. Lights Out was when the sun went down, for there was no artificial lighting in the Russian camp.

Ivan and his comrades mostly sat about waiting for something to happen, in the manner to which Russians are so well accustomed. You saw many men expertly darning socks; others spent hours watching the long-haired and mini-skirted youth of Prague go by, or writing letters home. But most of them stood or sat, in attitudes of ultimate Chekovian boredom, perhaps thinking of their homes far away, perhaps wondering when the counter-revolutionaries would strike, perhaps just sitting.

A clear distinction has to be drawn between what happened in the first two or three days of wild shooting and indefensible overkill, or at least overdemolish, and what happened afterwards. In the first hectic scenes, unforgettably reported blow-by-blow on the Czechoslovak television, the Russians killed some twenty people in Prague, shot up the airport, the national museum, the television centre, the Chinese embassy, and wrecked the premises of the Czech Writers Union after they arrived—with crowbars—to search for counter-revolutionary literature.

In one incident, which I cannot confirm, but which I think quite probable, Russian and Bulgarian units got entangled and shot it out, with some bloodshed. But the Red Army quickly returned to its reputation as one of the best disciplined armies in the world. I rate them close to the Israeli Army in this respect. I know of no authenticated case of rape or looting of private property, and with an army of more than half a million men, this is quite an achievement.

Ivan was very short of money. He was paid nothing in Czech crowns—another indication, perhaps, that this was a hastily prepared intervention—and he found his roubles very hard to change. The Soviet State Bank had issued long-standing instructions to the Czech banks not to change roubles for crowns, and the Czechs willingly carried out these orders during the occupation. A red star cap badge fetched, on the informal market in souvenirs which rapidly grew up, one packet of Czech cigarettes. There were some reports of money disappearing from public buildings occupied by the Russians—the safe at the television centre, for instance, had been forced and 37,000 crowns (about £1,000, $2,400, at a realistic rate) was missing. But these cases were probably the work of some junior commander, using his initiative to prepare for any eventuality. And even £1,000, shared out among a regiment of 1,200 men, is hardly pocket money.

The Russian purchases in Prague were modest and were not helped by the rumours which flooded the city to the effect that the Russians had issued the army of occupation with forged Czech money. Two soldiers came to my hotel and bashfully bought two litres of beer. Sometimes a patrol stopped at a bakery and emerged with a loaf of bread each, neatly wrapped in copies of a clandestine Czech newspaper. The most ambitious purchase I saw was that of a Soviet officer who bought a new pair of shoes with Czech money.

The Red Army was an authentic fighting formation occupying a cultivated Middle European city. The life of Ivan, camping out in the parks on his meagre rations, seemed all the more austere in contrast with the Prague bars and night clubs, reopened after a few days.

If the rations of the Russian troops were monotonous, so was their reading. *Pravda* and *Izvestia* were delivered promptly, and Ivan used them for his endless discussions with the Czechs. The system of political commissars seems to have been abandoned by the Soviet Army; at least, in the numberless political discussions to which I listened, no one took a leading role and the ordinary soldiers spoke up for themselves. There was of course, an immense amount of common ground. Many Russians are Slavs too; in theory at least, every Czech studies Russian at school, and until this year, Czechoslovaks and Russians lived under practically identical systems. The Russians clearly had orders to be firm but friendly, and I saw them take a lot of abuse from the Czechs—'Fascist' and the like. There were two or three stock questions: Were the Russian troops invited to Czechoslovakia? Were they an army of occupation? Was there a genuine counter-revolutionary plot? And so on. 'If we were a real army of occupation, would we be sleeping on the ground while you sleep in your apartments every night? We would be in the best hotels' was a common Russian argument, to which I did not hear an effective Czech reply. All the Czech–Russian contacts which I saw were on the level of each side trying to put the other right on points of socialist doctrine.

There was no ordinary fraternization, no boy meets girl, no evenings out in the Czech night spots. But on the level of Ivan and his Czech counterparts there was undoubtedly some sort of dialogue getting under way.

10 DUBCEK

Alexander Dubcek—'Sacha' to his family and friends —is a man with a sense of humour. About his own rise to power he has quipped: 'The people were dissatisfied with the Party leadership. We couldn't change the people—so we changed the leaders.' And now he too, the leader, changeth. Time only will tell whether that jest will turn sour in his mouth. But Dubcek (the name means 'little oak' in Russian), the tall, lean, stoop-shouldered and humble Slovak who at his first public speech as First Secretary of the Czechoslovak Communist Party, stammered through a prepared text that left people yawning, has become a real oak. He has grown into the job. From a mere Czechoslovak Party official he has sprung overnight into prominence, focus of the eyes of the whole world, both Communist and 'capitalistic'.

Said one diplomat in Prague: 'Dubcek is stubborn as only a Slovak can be. His backbone gets stiffer as the situation gets stickier.' His speeches have become much more effective. At the start of a crucial television address just one month before the invasion, his 'Dear friends, dear citizens' swept the country off its feet.

Brought up in Russia, and a graduate on a return visit many years later (in 1958) of the Communist Party Political College in Moscow, he is known to be fond of Russia and Russians. But his defiance of the Kremlin took the Russians by surprise.

At forty-six he became one of the youngest men ever to lead a Communist country. Still he shunned the trappings which usually identify top Communists in Eastern Europe. He has refused to seal himself off from the people and has appeared in newspaper photographs in bathing trunks—something unheard of in Iron Curtain countries. Unlike other Communist leaders, who have isolated themselves like idols in forbidden temples, Dubcek has allowed the people to see the real man, and not just the distant silhouette of the mighty oak.

He loves hunting, watching ice hockey, and is an ardent soccer fan. As a Slovak, there is an emotional side to his nature and he has been known to cry when his team, Bratislava, has lost. When at weekends he is able to drive the 200 miles from Prague to his home in Bratislava, he often turns up at the public swimming pool where he can perform a graceful dive. As children clamour for autographs he sits among them, cross-legged on the ground. And he carries a notebook to record the complaints and suggestions people offer him. At football matches he is often cheered longer than the players.

Politics is a passion with Sacha Dubcek. But to him that means working for the people. Even now that he is at the top of the ladder in Czechoslovak Communism, home is still a flat at 46 Mouse Street, on the outskirts of picturesque Bratislava, nestling in a curve of the River Danube near the Austrian border. His blonde, plump wife Anna answers the doorbell and queues for groceries instead of using the 'commissaries' for officials. Unlike the wives of other Party officials, she does not have a maid; just a charlady three mornings a week.

The Dubceks have three sons—Paul, 21, studies medicine; Peter, 18, and Milan, 15, attend the local secondary school. The family share their modest home with Alexander Dubcek's mother: his parents are divorced and his father lives in Trencin.

Dubcek's home is hung with souvenirs of his hunting forays. Said his mother, pointing to a large bearskin rug: 'For years this bear had been terrorizing a whole valley. Many famous hunters tried to kill it, but only my son, with characteristic patience, kept on.' In 1966 he succeeded; all the local papers reported it but the hunter's name was kept secret.

In spire-studded Prague Dubcek does not stay in Novotny's palatial apartment in Prague Castle; the Dubceks have a modest flat which he leaves around 7 a.m. every morning for his office in the huge granite Party headquarters on the banks of the Vltava. He began working eighteen hours a day on his reforms, and at crisis points slept only two hours a night—he soon lost twenty-eight pounds in weight. He ignores the official black Tatras and drives his own rather battered Simca, queues for petrol, and pays for it himself.

Alexander Dubcek is a second generation Communist. His father, Stefan Dubcek, a Slovak, lived in Budapest and was involved in the trade union movements of Austria–Hungary before World War I. In 1911 he emigrated to the United States. After taking out his papers as an American citizen in 1916, he found himself called up for military service. So he escaped into Mexico. But civil war in Mexico sent him scurrying back into the United States, where he was caught, fined $1000 and sent to jail for eighteen months. After his release he went to Chicago to work as a cabinet-maker with a firm of piano-makers at $25 a week. Early in 1920 the first of his two sons, Julius, was born at the modest Dubcek home on Madison Street, near Lincoln Park.

Stefan Dubcek, attracted by the prospects of the new, united, democratic Czechoslovakia, was persuaded to return to Slovakia, to the tiny village of Uhrovec. There, three months later, on November 27, 1921, Alexander Dubcek was born, in the small white-washed cottage which had been the home of a famous nineteenth century Slovak national hero, poet and liberal politician, Ludovik Stur.

Shortly after Alexander's birth, Stefan Dubcek, embittered by the difficult conditions persisting in Slovakia, became a pioneering member of the Czechoslovak Communist Party. In 1925 he moved once more with his family to found the Interhelpo co-operative in virgin lands of the Kirgiz steppe of Asiatic Russia, along with 300 other Czech and Slovak Communists. Stefan Dubcek, who had joined the Socialist Party of Illinois (Communist) in 1917, was one of the leaders of the group. Later most of them were purged by Stalin for 'cosmopolitan tendencies'. But Stefan had already returned in 1938 to Slovakia to organize the clandestine Communist Party, a job he carried out most diligently.

Brought up for thirteen years in Russia, almost on the Chinese border, Stefan's son Alexander could speak Russian as well as Slovak. But the qualifications he had gained at school in Frunze and Gorki were not recognized in Slovakia, so at eighteen he became an apprentice machine locksmith at the Skoda armaments factory at Dubnica, up the valley from Trencin. Ostensibly the family lived at Trencin, but Stefan was wanted by the police for his Communist activities, and was continually on the move. He was arrested in 1943 and sent to a concentration camp until the liberation.

Czechoslovakia's parliamentary democracy ended with the Munich Pact of 1938 and the subsequent German invasion. Alexander joined the illegal Czechoslovak Communist Party, and by night worked as a courier for the resistance. When the Slovak uprising began on August 28, 1944, he took to the Tatra Mountains with the Jan Zizka brigade, named after the most brilliant of the Hussite military commanders against the Germans five hundred years earlier. In an attempted ambush of a German Army detachment, his brother Julius was killed on New Year's Day, 1945, and Alexander was himself twice wounded in the right leg. One of the first things he did on coming to power was to award a supplementary pension to the peasant who sheltered and nursed him.

With the liberation he was reunited with his bride, a peasant's daughter who had risked her life smuggling food to German-held Russian prisoners; they went to live in Trencin, and Alexander worked for four years in a yeast factory. He was still practically unknown when in 1949 his father appealed for Alexander to be admitted to a Party career. He was chosen, mainly on the basis of his Russian background, and so began his slow, patient and determined climb as an *'apparatchik'* through the Party apparatus.

In his first Party job as Secretary for Trencin he had to nationalize local industries. Although this was 1949, the Stalinist era, and the first year of the Communist takeover in Czechoslovakia, Dubcek was firm with the factory owners, but *never* brutal. One whom he encouraged to return to university is now one of the country's most distinguished chemists. Two years later Dubcek became a candidate member of the Slovak Communist Party Central Committee, and in 1953 the leading regional secretary in Banska Bystrica.

His career suffered a setback in 1955 when he was not re-elected to the Central Committee and was removed from his Banska Bystrica post—some say because he was too lenient. But he got a scholarship to study law in Moscow, and graduated with honours (although this hardly compares with a university degree).

On his return from Moscow his promotion was rapid. In May 1958 he became a full member of the Slovak Central Committee, and a candidate member of the

Praesidium; in the same year he became a member of the C.C.P. Central Committee. As Kruschev pushed his anti-Stalinist campaign, Novotny was forced to drop some of the more notorious Stalinists from Czech Communist leadership. Dubcek benefited by becoming, in 1959, Regional Secretary for Bratislava in place of the ousted arch-Stalinist Karol Bacilek. By 1960 he had moved to Prague as Secretary of the Czechoslovak Central Committee, and two years later, at forty, he became one of the select ten on the Praesidium. At the same time he spent many terms as deputy of both the National Assembly and the Slovak National Council.

In 1963, when Novotny was forced to sack the vicious secret policeman he had made First Secretary of the Slovak Communist Party, the post went to Dubcek—the 6ft. 4in. blue-eyed blond, with long nose and puckish smile, who has come to be known by Slovak and Czech alike as 'Our Alexander the Great'.

Dubcek is a proud Slovak and loyal to those aggrieved little people, the 'Scots of Czechoslovakia' (some $4\frac{1}{2}$ million in a population of fourteen million). He often went back to Trencin at week-ends, and the town remained loyal to him. It was the Trencin Party in fact which first publicly called for Novotny's resignation in 1967.

As First Secretary in Slovakia, Dubcek allowed Slovak writers and intellectuals sensational freedom. The crimes of Stalinism were assailed in Bratislava while Prague was still silent. In September 1967 Dubcek complained publicly that Slovakia was not getting enough money to develop its resources and that investments allotted for the area from the central fund should be increased to 28 per cent. He also identified himself with the new economic theories of Professor Ota Sik and his colleagues. Thus Dubcek forged the alliance between the Slovaks and the reformers which led, after an intense and bitter struggle, to Antonin Novotny's downfall.

Few had suspected how mighty would become that 'little oak'. And, chuckled Stefan Dubcek, who at 76 was still looking after the Slovak National Council's personnel records: 'When my boy was at the Political College in Moscow, Novotny, who was then First Secretary of the Party, came to Bratislava. I asked him how Alexander was getting on. Novotny said: "Alexander is doing extremely well. He is the best of his class this year. I predict he will go far in the party." '

On March 23, the struggle for power between Novotny's Stalinist wing, and the liberal wing, represented by Dubcek, was over. Novotny resigned from his post as President of the Socialist Republic of Czechoslovakia.

Within his first months as First Secretary, Alexander Dubcek took the country by storm: he was a popular leader—the first the country had had in twenty years of Communism—who gained massive public support by his honesty and integrity; and, as a Czech politician said, 'he is not power hungry'.

Dubcek seems genuinely to want his countrymen to have a greater voice in their affairs—within six months of his election 30,000 new members joined the Socialist Party, one of the five minority parties in Czechoslovakia which until Dubcek could not have more than 20,000 members. The estimated membership of the Communist Party throughout Czechoslovakia is 1,700,000.

Within his first hundred days of power, Czechoslovakia had become the most liberal of Communist states. Freedom of expression reigned; in March the Czechoslovaks had their first strike under Communism, at an electrical appliance factory in Pisek; police were required to wear numbered badges for identification; three top secretaries of the central Trade Union Council were forced to quit, as was the boss of the Women's

Union; the judiciary undertook to review cases heard during the purges of the 1950s to right injustices; the Church was freed of retraints; rehabilitation began of the thousands of victims of Stalinist purges; the National Assembly was to be given real legislative powers. Dubcek urged the re-writing of Czechoslovakia's laws to allow secret balloting, the right to emigrate and travel abroad, and the freedom of national groups such as students' associations, farmers and unions from Party ties. Key posts in the economy and Government were opened to non-Party members, and political detention was abolished.

Above all, Alexander Dubcek was trying to apply the Marxist principle that in practising socialism every Party must respect the traditions and conditions of its country.

People who know him well say he has an even temper and knows how to handle people; that he is cautious, shrewd, rather calculating, but infinitely opposed to the use of force—a persuader. Several times he warned against extremism: 'Democracy must include discipline. Rules must be accepted and kept by everyone.'

As wave after wave of crises hit his country, Dubcek showed courage, steel, and sober calm; he injected the nation with calm. He reaffirmed his belief in the international brotherhood of socialist countries. But he alarmed his hard-line neighbours with the huge success of his reforms, because they feared a spillover effect might result in demands for liberalization all round.

On July 27, within hours of meeting the Russians, he declared to his people: 'I should like to assure you that we shall act in such a way that at any time we can with clear conscience render account of our deeds to all of you whom we represent. We can already say that a unity has been created such as there has not been for many years.'

'He is the saviour of our nation', said a starry-eyed

youth at Bratislava, where great crowds waited five hours to greet him with an explosion of cheers and applause after the Bratislava talks. Letters of appreciation poured into radio, television and the press from all groups and classes of people. The Czechoslovak Journalists' Association said in a message that the Praesidium 'enjoys such confidence as no leadership of our country has had in the past fifty years'.

The rise of Alexander Dubcek was no mere accident. He has been a professional politician for twenty years. Born a Communist and bred a Communist throughout the Stalinist era, he nevertheless has assumed none of the rigidity of that breed and abhors the 'discredited bureaucratic-police method' leadership. He proposes to work by consent, rather than by dictatorship; yet he is a man of great determination and perseverance.

Another clue to his personality is to be found in a phrase from his first major policy speech in which he said it was important 'to probe all problems soberly, factually, boldly, and, above all, with consideration.'

Dubcek is a Party believer. He is also a believer in true socialism and democracy. And in its profoundest sense, it may be said that he is also deeply religious: he is probably the first Communist leader in the Western bloc since Lenin to try sincerely to live in a Communist way, rejecting not only the privileges and trappings of power, but also the isolation. Honesty, humanism, internationalism and peace are his gods; and he lives as he preaches.

As the days rolled on from August 21 to September 21, Russian pressure against him grew, in an attempt to bring about his resignation or—even more effective— to discredit him in the eyes of his people, thereby sowing the seeds of destruction in the unity and courage of their resistance. But Dubcek, tired and battered, spurred by his deep idealism and the faith of the Czechoslovaks, drove on. His refusal to allow the agenda for the Moscow talks to include a list of people the Russians wanted the Czechs to arrest was one of the main reasons for postponing the Czechoslovak leaders' visit to Moscow, first planned for September 20. And the Russians want Dubcek himself to order the arrests: nothing would more surely destroy Dubcek's popular following.

Dubcek, gentle, saintly, with a strong compassion for humanity, and a profound instinct for and belief in the preservation of his nation, was the perfect leader for the glorious months of freedom. But several Czechoslovak leaders say that his intense idealism is tinged with naïveté, and that he is not the best leader for the duel with the Russians. For him to resign would be a grave setback for national morale; but there are other politicians waiting in the wings.

The alternative leaders most mentioned are Dr Gustav Husak, First Secretary of the Slovak Communist Party (the post formerly held by Dubcek), and Mr Mlynar, the C.C.P's theoretician in Prague. Or else, it is thought, a compromise might be reached with the Russians in which Dubcek would nominally keep his post, with Husak and Mlynar as leaders of semi-autonomous Czech and Slovak regions under the federalization scheme planned to operate from October 28, 1968.

Dr Husak, small, rather charmless and cold-mannered, is untypical of the somewhat impulsive and open-hearted Slovaks. Yet he is, above all, a Slovak nationalist, and immensely ambitious. Born in Bratislava in 1913, he trained as a lawyer, was in the forefront of the Slovak uprising of 1944 against the Germans and became a national hero. For a short time after the war he was Slovak Prime Minister until imprisoned by Novotny, more for his Slovak sentiments than suspected liberalism. Indeed, Husak received his Communist training in the Stalinist period of the 1930s and 1940s and remains an orthodox Party man. He was released from prison in 1960, and this year made a political comeback as one of the three Deputy Premiers in Prague under Cernik, and more recently as a member of the Praesidium and as Slovak First Secretary.

It is possible that he is jealous of Dubcek who, nearly ten years his junior, has stolen his limelight as the noblest Slovak of them all. As a group of Slovak students said: 'We want badly to trust Husak—we wish we could.'

Mr Mlynar has been called a political weathervane. However, his ideology seems to be pointing in a liberal direction at the moment. Under Novotny he was charged with defining long-term perspectives for the future of the Party, and it was his ideas, many of them very progressive, that formed much of the basis of Dubcek's Action Programme.

Since he wants to transform Czechoslovak society within the bounds of socialism, Alexander Dubcek may be compared with the fifteenth-century Czech theologian Jan Hus, who tried to reform the Roman Catholic Church from within, but saw his followers break away and form their own movement, while Hus was burnt at the stake.

Dubcek's position in Czechoslovakia may also depend on his ability to stand up to Soviet pressure; if he fails, he could find himself attacked by his own people who are overwhelmingly (more than 80 per cent according to a recent survey) in favour of reforming their country's way of life.

11 WHY?

Gradually the free radio stations and the bold, liberal newspapers and magazines were snuffed out. One by one their lights grew dim, and faded, like the gas lanterns of an old city. And a darkness began to spread, almost evilly, over Czechoslovakia, as the rays of hope that had been there before August 21, that had somehow survived while Dubcek, Cernik and his colleagues bargained at the big man's table in the Kremlin, vanished, perhaps not for good, but until a new battle could be fought. Those who had been in the forefront of organizing the clandestine radio were dismissed from their posts. One well known Czechoslovak journalist wrote:

'Up to the moment when we heard President Svoboda's speech and the Moscow communique we were, in spite of all the tanks, a nation free and unconquered. Only at that moment did we become crushed.'

On September 6 the last 'free edition' of *Kulturny Zivot* (*Cultural Life*), was written, published and clandestinely distributed. This Bratislava weekly was one of the early forces behind the whole Czechoslovak progressive movement. It was the magazine on which Dr Gustav Husak, the new Slovak Party Secretary in Bratislava worked until, two months before the invasion, he decided it was too progressive and walked out with some colleagues and started his own *Nove Slovo*.

At a meeting of the Union of Slovak Writers it was decided to take a final opportunity to make a published statement on the invasion and its aftermath. The *Kulturny Zivot* works were under guard, but the Red Army had omitted to seize the offices of the official Slovak Communist daily, *Bratislava Pravda*. No doubt the Russians were under the false impression that a newspaper with the name *Pravda* must be connected with their own *Pravda* in Moscow, that it was friendly to them, and anyway sacrosanct. The outcome was that the *Kulturny Zivot* publishers were able to make use of the unguarded *Pravda* composing room, and the 'free issue' came off the presses there.

Copies were much fewer than usual, because the

staff did not want to keep the presses running too long, for fear that a Russian security man would arrive. Members of the staff took armfuls of copies, and gave them out by hand in the streets. Some took their cars full of the papers to towns and villages. Many of the contributors were writing just as defiantly as they were before the invasion. Bohuslav Graca is one of the leading Communists of Slovakia, the Central Committee Secretary in charge of ideology, but he declared himself as being firmly against the Moscow agreement on the grounds that the Czechoslovak leaders had to negotiate it under duress. Pavol Stevcek was chief editor of *Kulturny Zivot* until 1964 when he was dismissed by Novotny and harassed by him until he suffered a heart attack. He had just been elected a member of the new Central Committee, but that gave him no qualms about writing: 'The question is not that the Russians killed dozens of innocent people. It is that they have now given orders for their blood to be washed off the pavements.' Poignantly dramatist Peter Karvas wrote: 'sense, unity, Svoboda, Dubcek, Husak, hope'.

Why did the Russians do it? Were the displays of sincerity and the bear hugs at Bratislava just an act, or did the leaders of the Kremlin change their minds once they had got back to Moscow and heard that the liberal reformist movement was travelling so fast.

Some believe that the Kremlin always intended to invade Czechoslovakia, but first felt obliged to placate world opinion somewhat. Having reached an agreement, it would then be open to them to say that the Czechoslovaks had breached it.

Picking over what little evidence is available and discussing the Kremlin's ponderings and final action with diplomats and experts on Soviet affairs brings me to the conclusion that Moscow decided several months before the invasion that she would have to rescue Czechoslovakia from what she considered to be the perils of 'counter-revolution', and planned to intervene by using military force. The Russian leaders had genuine second thoughts during negotiations held at Cierna, but never took their armed forces off the alert during this time. In fact the Red Army and other Warsaw Pact troops had been waiting for the invasion call from the day in early July that Defence Minister Marshal Andrei Grechko hurried back from Algiers.

But the decision to invade was sudden. The Soviet Central Committee met specially six hours before the invasion began, and Leonid Breshnev, Kosygin and Podgorny were all suddenly recalled from their holidays.

It seems possible that the agreements reached at Cierna and Bratislava may have been accepted by a majority of the Soviet Politburo but not by the Central Committee, or, if so, only by a slender margin of its members. Perhaps they decided that the action taken was not good enough; that Kosygin and Breshnev had not waved their 'Warsaw Letter' of July 15 sufficiently hard in Dubcek's face. And they certainly knew they were up against time, for the Czechoslovak Communist Party Congress was due to take place on September 9, and the outcome of the Cierna and Bratislava agreements would then have been publicly ratified, making it harder than ever for Moscow to force the Czechs and Slovaks to toe the line. The Party Congress—had it been held—would certainly have meant the end of the road for Novotny supporters.

It came as a great shock for Moscow when the military commanders and the diplomats reported that they could not raise any worthwhile support, either in the Party Central Committee, the Praesidium, or amongst the people. Most of the Russian soldiers had been led to believe that Dubcek was supported only by a minority of revisionist hotheads, and therefore found it hard to understand why there were violently anti-Soviet slogans painted on almost every wall and hoarding. Older soldiers with greater knowledge, perhaps even recollections, of the horrors of the war with Germany, were deeply hurt that a nation of people considered to be their friends should be publicly comparing them with jackbooted Nazis.

The fear of Germany in the invasion calculations was underlined by Polish diplomats in Prague who complained that the repeated visits of many West German bankers and politicians to the Czechoslovak capital in the early summer was evidence that the Americans and the Germans were 'buying' the country. One East German writer put it to an American journalist this way: 'The invasion was completely necessary. Had it not taken place, Czechoslovakia would have gone over to your side in eight to ten months, upsetting the balance of power and making real trouble for you and the Soviet Union.'

Moscow has, of course, always been concerned about losing the 'dagger in the heart of Europe', or as Bismark once put it, the 'Bohemian fortress triangle'. After Dubcek returned from detention at his tense marathon meeting in Moscow with the Kremlin leaders, he admitted that he and his colleagues had underestimated the strategic and military importance Moscow placed on Czechoslovakia, and it was clear the Prague reformers had failed to take into account that Communist leaders in East Berlin, Warsaw and Budapest had been panicked by the growing new *détente* between the Czechs and the Germans.

Mr Jiri Hajek, the Foreign Minister, had laid great emphasis on improving future relations with Bonn when he visited Budapest, East Berlin and other East European capitals before the invasion and, as a result, failed to convince the Kremlin leaders that Czechoslovakia would stay in the Warsaw Pact. They saw in him another version of West German Foreign Minister,

Willi Brandt, an apostle of European unity. There is no doubt that Russia realized that the Communist powers cannot yet stand the test of integration, and that is why de Gaulle's one Europe from the Atlantic to the Urals is likely to remain a dream long after his death.

What Hajek actually said was that Prague would support East Germany all the way on its claims to full sovereign recognition, but would reserve its right as an independent state to work out its foreign policy with West Germany. This was too much for the Kremlin, and anathema to Ulbricht in East Berlin. Russia had encouraged the Czechs to look for economic help from West Germany under Novotny, but as soon as his hard liners were replaced by Mr Dubcek and his followers, dealings with Bonn were regarded by them as particularly sinister. I am inclined to believe that Russian fears about Czechs fraternizing with West Germans were not unjustified. Since the beginning of 1968 there had been a very close link between Czech factory managers and West German businessmen, following the establishment of a trade delegation in Prague. The delegation consisted of twenty people—drivers and tea-makers included. There were five executives—quasi-diplomats—and they lived in a smooth suite in the Hotel Yalta in Wenceslas Square. Dubcek's Government had promised them an 'embassy', publicly described more tactfully as an 'office'.

* * *

In March 1921 the soldiers and sailors of the garrison at Kronstadt, near Leningrad, rebelled against the Communist Government of the Soviet Union. They demanded, amongst other things, immediate free elections by secret ballot; freedom of speech for workers, peasants, and all pro-socialist political parties; the freeing of all political prisoners; the abolition of secret trials and the Communist terror detachments in the Army and in the villages; freedom for trade unions to negotiate wages and conditions directly with the only employer, the State; and freedom for the peasants in the use of the land.

These demands are eerily similar to Dubcek's Action Programme of 1968. The mood of Russia in 1921 was, in fact, strikingly similar to that of Czechoslovakia. The soldiers and sailors of Kronstadt had, along with many Russians, supported the Bolsheviks because they promised peace, bread and land. Instead, they found that Communist rule meant police terror, and dictatorship by the Communist Party, which claimed (and still claims) to be 'the vanguard of the working class'. The Tenth Congress of the All-Union Communist Party branded the Kronstadt rebellion as 'counter-revolution' as it still figures in Soviet history books, and the Red Army was ordered into the attack. After heavy fighting most of the rebels were killed, and the survivors were later executed. The process of stifling discussion, even inside the Party, of concentrating power in fewer and fewer hands, went on, and culminated in the nightmarish dictatorship of Stalin. And most of the delegates who ordered the suppression of this first 'counter-revolution' themselves perished in Stalin's great purges.

Was there a genuine counter-revolution at Kronstadt in the sense that the rebels wanted the Czar back, or the reconstruction of Russian capitalism? No, there was none. It was the challenge to the monolithic rule of the Communist Party, ultimately to become the rule of one man, which alarmed the Party Congress into brutal action. The fact that the rebels were also on the left, which seems so important to a non-Communist, made no difference; in fact, the threat from the left seemed more dangerous.

The Bolshevik revolution of 1917 was made in the name of freedom, democracy and majority rule. The principles are central to Marxism itself, and as long as Communists go on reading Marx, these demands will keep coming forward—if, indeed, they do not spring directly from human nature itself. Marx argued that capitalism and imperialism destroyed the natural bonds between man and man; that money values took the place of human values; that men were dehumanized, and could not reach anything like their true stature as human beings. Socialism, in the end, meant freedom, the conditions in which men could truly begin to live as brothers.

But the Bolshevik revolution was not made by a majority. In fact, their first move was to smash an elected Government. In 1917 Russia was a backward country, devastated by war. There were millions of peasant soldiers in uniform, but hardly any 'working class' in the sense in which Marx thought of them, an industrial proletariat exploited by capitalism. In strict Marxist theory, the revolution was impossible.

Lenin improvised the conditions for a revolution. To the peasants, he promised land. They thought this meant that they would own it, to do what they liked with it; to Lenin it meant that the State would own it. All power, he promised, would go to the working class. The Communist Party was to be the 'vanguard' of the Russian 'working class', a dictatorship to continue only until the working class had developed to the point at which it could take over power. In fact, the rule of the Communist 'vanguard' goes on to this day. Most members of the Soviet Communist Party are not 'workers'; they are managers, foremen, intellectuals—the Soviet Establishment.

Murray Sayle and I discussed this, and we believe the Czech affair shows that the doctrine of the vanguard has not changed, despite the genuine liberalization which has taken place in the Soviet Union in recent years. On the face of things there is nothing in the

Czech Action Programme which is against Marxist doctrine; in fact, every one of the Czech proposals would be welcomed by many people, probably a majority in the Soviet Union itself.

The occupation of Czechoslovakia shows that the Russian Communists think they are still the vanguard, not only of the Russian working class, but of the working class of all the Communist countries of Eastern Europe, or for that matter the working class of the whole world.

A Czech friend of Murray Sayle in Prague, a member and functionary of the C.C.P. for twenty years, put the situation succinctly: 'We Communists have been talking all our lives about the irreconcilable conflicts in capitalism and imperialism which will infallibly tear those systems apart. What about conflicts in socialism?

'Dubcek, Smrkovsky, Cernik and the rest of our leaders—even General Svoboda—are all Communists. They have all been talking for years about socialism leading to freedom and democracy. In the time of the Novotny dictatorship they continued to talk about these objectives, and like good Communists to work for them as well. And when we got rid of Novotny by peaceful methods, we thought why not us? Why not now?'

What the Russians want in Czechoslovakia, as they keep saying, is 'a normal socialist life'. This means to them rule by the Communist Party, unshared with any other parties or social groupings. The C.C.P. was gaining steadily in popularity by showing itself ready to share power with other well-intentioned organizations. Not much power had, in fact, been shared out, but to the Russians any weakening of the 'vanguard' role opened the way to chaos, in which genuine counter-revolutionaries might emerge and even seize power.

Last April Breshnev circulated to closed meetings of the Soviet Party's twelve million members, a report from the Party Plenum that there was a serious danger developing that Czechoslovakia might leave the

Communist camp altogether, and that 'we are ready to go to any lengths to stop this happening'. This danger seemed absurd to Czechoslovak Communists, but it alarmed the Russians into the grave move of military intervention, which might have shed more blood but for the discipline and unity of the Czechs.

Murray Sayle, with first hand, on-the-spot experience of the occupation period, says confidently that there were no counter-revolutionaries of any consequence at all in Czechoslovakia. Far from trying to destroy socialism, the Czechoslovaks thought they were improving it, and this is what alarmed the Russians most. Above all, they were disturbed by what they called 'hostile attacks on the Soviet Union' in the newly free press. Our Czech friend said: 'Of course there was criticism in the free press. Writers in our newspapers were even criticizing their editors. You would expect, surely, to see criticism in every direction in a free press wouldn't you? The Russians are frightened of freedom, not because they are against it, but because they have never tried it.'

But the Russians did not see it this way. If any experimenting is to be done in the Communist system, they want to do it themselves. Add Russian uneasiness about Germany, which has at least good historical reasons, and the background against which the fateful decision to invade was made becomes clear.

The Russians cannot, of course, be so frank about their motives. Bereft of explanation for the invasion which could be freely given to their own people, they have been reduced to implausible accounts of having been invited into Czechoslovakia by people there who were worried about the turn of events—who?—or of caches of hidden arms, gangs of dangerous counter-revolutionaries, or plots by Western Imperialists.

In covering the Czech crisis both of us found some hopeful elements in a generally gloomy picture. The loss of life was deplorable but it was, by the standards of such operations, surprisingly small. The Czechs are already beginning to look back on the period between January and August 21, 1968, as a sort of golden age, and legends—inevitably, they tend to be exaggerated—have a way of holding small embattled people together in adversity. 'I believe we had the freest press in the world here, freer than anything you have in the West' said a Czech journalist proudly.

Above all, the leaders who held the Czechoslovaks together in the early days of the occupation were all Communists. Communist and non-Communist Czechs co-operated freely and voluntarily. If a free and creative form of socialism does finally emerge in Eastern Europe, the Czech experience will have contributed much towards it.

Russia made a colossal blunder; there is a chance the Moscow leadership may come to recognize this, although they are of course unlikely to say so publicly for a very long time. But, terrible as the occupation was, some progress has been made: Prague in August 1968 was bad enough, but it was not as bad as Budapest in 1956, or Kronstadt in 1921.